Through a Mother's Eyes:
Hope and Healing on the Special Needs Journey

LISA J. PLETT

©2024 by Lisa J. Plett

Published by hope*books
2217 Matthews Township Pkwy
Suite D302
Matthews, NC 28105
www.hopebooks.com

hope*books is a division of hope*media

Printed in the United States of America

All rights reserved. Without limiting the rights under copyrights reserved above, no part of this publication may be scanned, uploaded, reproduced, distributed, or transmitted in any form or by any means whatsoever without express prior written permission from both the author and publisher of this book—except in the case of brief quotations embodied in critical articles and reviews.

Thank you for supporting the author's rights.

First paperback edition.
Paperback ISBN: 979-8-89185-098-9
Hardcover ISBN: 979-8-89185-099-6
Ebook ISBN:979-8-89185-100-9
Library of Congress Number :2024941955

All Bible references use the Holy Bible, New Living Translation,(NLT) copyright © 1996, 2004, 2015 by Tyndale House Foundation. Used by permission of Tyndale House Publishers, Inc., Carol Stream, Illinois 60188. All rights reserved.

Praise for In A Stroke of Love

"Lisa, a young sweet mother, finds herself navigating an unforeseen situation while searching for what God has for her life. She shares her journey with her special needs son through honest and authentic storytelling. This book will be an invaluable resource for parents of special needs children, helping them connect with their emotions. It provides profound insights for professionals in the disability field and a meaningful guide for family and friends to better understand and support their loved ones."

—***Elizabeth Clawson***, MS, PhD, LCP, HSPP

"Lisa wrote from her heart, and this book affected and impacted me in ways I didn't anticipate. Though my journey differs in details from the authors, the emotions and experiences are very real and similar. For anyone finding themselves in a tough spot, facing a hard journey, this book is a must-read. For special needs moms, it will make you cry and laugh. You will feel, as I did, every emotion that Lisa experienced. Your soul will resonate with every page, and I believe you can find hope and healing through this book."

—***Vicki Witmer***, Special Needs Mom

"In a Stroke of Love is a beautifully written and thought-provoking story. Its details reveal a strength, love, and tenacity unlike any I've ever seen before. It turns out moms are superheroes—but we already knew that."

—***Clarence Hogan***, Pastor

Contents

Introduction vii

Chapter 1 –Framework 1

Chapter 2 –The Defining Moment 13

Chapter 3 –Comparison and Denial 23

Chapter 4 –All Things Medical and Therapy 35

Chapter 5 –Family Ties 53

Chapter 6 –Special Education 65

Chapter 7 –Another Life Changing Diagnosis 81

Chapter 8 –The Divine Call that Broke Me 93

Chapter 9 –Normal Please 105

Chapter 10 –It Takes a Village 113

Chapter 11 –Identity 123

Chapter 12 –On Board the Grief Train 131

Chapter 13 –Caregiving and Burnout 143

Chapter 14 –Letting Go 153

Chapter 15 –Hope and Healing 169

Acknowledgements 177

Endnotes 181

Introduction

It was 2008, and I received a divine calling from God to write a book. The title of the book came to me right away: *In a Stroke of Love*. I started putting my thoughts and memories to paper. At the heart of this endeavor was my son Bryson, ten years old at the time. Reflecting on my perceived wealth of knowledge, I believed I had much to share. Little did I know that 15 years would pass before the culmination of this book, a testament to the transformative journey that has unfolded since I heard the call.

This memoir covers a journey marked with trials, questions, and unexpected turns. What transpired in the past 26 years has molded me into the person I am today, and for that, I am profoundly grateful. The process of writing these pages has been a rollercoaster of emotions – exciting, heart-wrenching, and above all, healing. As I present my story to the world, it is indeed a dream realized.

Throughout the book, you will witness the perfect orchestration of God's timing. I don't totally understand the timing, but He knows. He knew that I would receive an email from Hope*Books in the week after a life-changing event with Bryson. He knew that I would need time for grieving and healing to embrace the new life chapter. Writing this book emerged as a crucial component of my personal healing journey during this time.

As you delve into the stories woven within these pages, I hope you can recognize what God has taught me. Though our individual stories may differ, the threads of sadness, anger, grief, joy, and hope bind us all. It is my prayer that as you navigate my journey alongside me, you may draw inspiration from the lessons God imparted during my journey with Bryson. May you find resonance with your own experiences, embark on a journey of hope and healing, and embrace the profound truth of God's love for you!

CHAPTER 1
The Framework

> "The richness of a human experience would lose something of rewarding joy if there were no limitations to overcome. The hilltop hour would not be half as wonderful if there were no dark valleys to traverse."
>
> Helen Keller[1]

The hallway to my kindergarten class stretched like an endless corridor, and the unforgiving hum of the overhead fluorescent lights was silenced by the students' laughter, chatter, and occasional hushed whispers. "You are such a fatty," his words, dripping with laughter and sarcasm, lingered in my ears like a haunting melody. The memory of his piercing eyes, gleaming with mischief, etched itself into the canvas of my young mind.

These spoken words unfolded during the innocent days of kindergarten, where I, a chubby little girl, first encountered the sting of hurtful words. Not fully aware of the magnitude of that short phrase, those cutting remarks burrowed deep into the tender recesses of my heart.

From that day forward, the impact of that early teasing shaped my interactions with others. I felt inferior to my classmates, particularly boys, as I painted them with the same brush as the mischievous boy from kindergarten. In response, I retreated into my shyness. The rosy blush would stain my cheeks at the mere interaction with anyone outside of my trusted circle of friends. The thought of engaging in extracurricular activities or class participation sent shivers down my spine, fueled by the belief that everyone would make fun of me. Several classmates, noticing my uneasiness, seized opportunities to increase my discomfort, attempting to elicit that telltale flush of embarrassment.

Another classmate, an Amish girl, shared my disposition of shyness. Together, we became targets of teasing, a cruel game where classmates vied to see which one could induce the most intense blush. It was these early experiences that formed the foundation of insecurities and the relentless quest for acceptance in a world that, at times, seemed cruel. My weight and shyness made me NOT ENOUGH!

Growing up within the confines of a conservative church and nestled in an Amish community in Indiana, my world was painted with hues of tradition and rules. My attire was made up of dresses, skirts, culottes, and blouses. My mother, the diligent seamstress, crafted all my clothes with love, yet they bore no resemblance to the day's fashion. My long, uncut hair was worn in ponytails and pigtails, and my appearance rendered me distinctively different from the cool crowd that seemed to effortlessly blend in. My insecurities increased during gym classes. The stinging awareness of not being able to don the "regular" gym clothes heightened my discomfort.

In a state where basketball reigned supreme, I loved basketball. Even in the shyness, I had a competitive spirit and participated in a free throw contest in sixth grade. I won the girl's division and was invited to represent the school at regionals. However, the grandeur of the large crowds and vibrant cheers amplified my shyness and led to a poor performance. The reverberating sound of missed shots left me feeling like a failure. Even with this failure, I mustered the courage to join the 7th grade girls' basketball team the following year, only to withdraw after a mere two weeks. The fear of making a fool of myself, coupled with the discomfort of standing out in my culottes among teammates clad in shorts, overwhelmed me. Looking back, the girls on the team extended acceptance, yet my own insecurities blocked the opportunity to participate and make genuine connections.

This marked the inception of my role as a spectator rather than a participant in the world of sports. I became a fervent watcher, immersing myself in the love of the games while remaining on the sidelines, wary of the vulnerability that participation might expose. Being different fueled my lack of confidence and instilled fear, relegating me to the sidelines of life.

My childhood home, a sprawling, beautiful gray farmhouse, was close to a large, wooded area full of deer and other wildlife. The house featured a wraparound porch with a hunter-green porch swing looking over a pond. From there, you could see an island reached only by a white-arched wooden bridge. Across the well-manicured lawn sat a white trailer owned by my step-grandma Deary and my aunt, Joanna, who had Down Syndrome.

One afternoon, as I stepped off the school bus, I welcomed the warm spring fresh air, a change from the bus's lingering scent of sweaty kids. The walk up the lengthy driveway to my house was a routine I usually enjoyed, but other times I wished that our house was right beside the road. I decided to detour to Grandma Deary's trailer, a familiar stop along my path.

I gently tapped the screen door and heard, "Come in." Entering, I found Deary at the kitchen sink with Joanna beside her, occupied with drying dishes. Deary's signature strawberry trifle dessert sat on the table, a tempting sight after a day at school. As I settled into a nearby blue recliner, conversation flowed between Deary and me. I could sense Joanna was becoming irritated as Deary focused her attention on me; she became more aggressive in her drying.

Suddenly, a Tupperware lid sailed across the room, ricocheting off the arm of the recliner before landing on the floor. Deary, with her characteristic kindness, gently reprimanded Joanna for the gesture. However, Joanna's response was one of defiance as she retreated to her room in a huff. The atmosphere, once warm and welcoming, turned tense, and I knew it was best for me to leave.

Despite Deary's love for me, her inclination to side with Joanna and tolerate her behavior was normal. My connection with Joanna was entwined with jealousy as we both fought for Deary's affection. This harmless object, the Tupperware lid, served as a potent symbol of our ongoing conflict.

At thirteen, my life took an unexpected turn when Deary's battle against cancer came to a heart-wrenching end. Economic challenges loomed over the household during this time. The U.S. was in a recession, sending my mother into the workforce, working night shifts at a local nursing home. Joanna was my mother's sister, and my mother had assisted in her care for many years. It was clear the best place for Joanna, so as not to upset her life any more than losing her mother, was to come and live with us. Joanna's transition into our home unfolded against a backdrop of my increasing insecurities and the pressures of adolescence.

The ongoing battle between Joanna and me took a new turn and shifted from vying for Deary's attention to a silent contest for my mother's time. Our family, generally reserved, could feel the upheaval of strained emotions simmering beneath the surface. The impact of Joanna's presence stretched beyond the physical realm of our home; she had previously been involved in various handicap programs, and now, our family found itself forced into this new reality. Attending her programs and assisting in weekend retreats became obligations I reluctantly shouldered. Resentment towards Joanna deepened, casting a shadow over our interactions. The world that had already felt distinctively different to me now seemed even stranger as I became involved in the unfamiliar landscape of disabilities. One evening, as I lay scared and confused in my bed, I poured out a poignant plea to God. *"Anything but a handicapped child,"* I whispered, the weight of my words echoing in the stillness of the night. The disability world was scary, and I was confused.

My father, rooted in an Amish upbringing, and my mother, a preacher's kid from a conservative family, instilled in my brother, Nate, and me the importance of church, serving others, and having a strong faith in God. Our lives revolved around the happenings of our church, a commitment that saw us within the church walls whenever its doors were open - Sunday morning, Sunday evening, and Wednesday nights.

I learned the value of cultivating friendships within the church community, and my parents instilled the importance of these friendships. Despite the absence of girls my age, I forged meaningful connections with older peers, and to this day, my closest friends, Fran and Lynette, hail from those church-going days.

At the tender age of 14, a quiet yet insistent pressure began to weigh on me. As my friendships in the church were with older peers, I felt the need to do as they did. My friends had taken the step and were baptized and became members of the church. It wasn't the baptism part that slowed my decision; it was the church's requirement to wear the head covering at all times as a member that threatened the essence of who I was. The scriptures about the covering of the Lord echoed in my ears, but the resonance was hollow, failing to ignite a conviction within me.

The pivotal evening unfolded when I sought out my mother. She was sitting in the black leather chair in my father's study. His study was adorned with floor-to-ceiling bookshelves that housed the many books that my parents read and revered. "Mom, do you have a conviction for the head covering?" I asked. Her honesty resonated with authenticity. "Lisa, I wear it out of respect and headship to my husband. It's really all I know. I was raised this way, but I can't say I have a strong personal conviction." The power of her admission reverberated within me, and in that moment, a realization dawned: I didn't have a husband and my relationship with God need not be tethered to a piece of cloth.

Armed with this newfound clarity, I approached the preachers during one of the baptism classes and shared with them my conviction. I pledged to wear the covering to church, honoring that tradition but would not be bound to it throughout the week. To my surprise, they accepted this compromise, and I went through the ritual of baptism.

Yet, even as I received the pouring of water at baptism, I grappled with the true essence of this sacred act. I grasped the surface-level understanding of outwardly professing my faith, however the depth of the spiritual journey, understanding the deep love of my Heavenly Father, these remained elusive to my young and questioning mind.

The label of "rebel" began to whisper through the congregants, not uttered directly to my face, but a quiet unsettling wave of judgment settled on my shoulders. My heart, earnest and longing, struggled to reconcile with the rules and restrictions. Despite having expressed my desire to the leadership, I found myself defenseless against the words circulating about me, left to bear the weight of them in isolation.

My mother, a beacon of honesty and love, also bore the pressure of others' judgments about her daughter. She understood my questioning heart. When asked, "Why can my cousins wear pants, and I can't? If God loves them and He loves me, why does it matter?" my mother calmly replied, "It's ok Lisa, to be you. God loves you."

My father and I avoided discussing these matters; he allowed my mom to take the lead in these conversations. Recently, my mom recounted this poignant story to me. One Sunday morning, as my mom and dad were preparing for church in their bathroom, she opened up about her internal struggle with the decisions I was making. In that vulnerable moment, as she gazed into the mirror, my father responded with wisdom, saying, "If you want to remain her friend, don't put distance between you, that is what's important." These words served as a soothing balm to my soul, nurturing a deeper love and respect for my father.

During these years, I wore the covering only for church activities, and I ventured further into the "breaking the rules" zone when I cut my hair in the back and added feathered bangs. The act of cutting my hair introduced another level of tension in my home. This was not something I could easily conceal. Despite my awareness that my parents disapproved of this act, their love, a constant presence, stood unwavering. In the core of my being, I never identified as a rebel. I was merely pursuing that voice inside of me that wanted to believe God's love embraced me for who I was. Yet, the whispers behind closed doors, the conversations among certain ladies, bore the sting of judgment. The belief that people were always watching what I did left me wounded with the thought that I was not safe and not quite good enough for God.

As the years passed, I unconsciously told myself that my value would not be found in my appearance. The fervent need to discover where I could excel gnawed at the edges of my consciousness. The realization struck me - I excelled in school. Thus, my self-worth became intricately woven with my academic performance, propelling me into a relentless pursuit of perfection throughout my school years.

With unyielding determination, I dived deep into my studies, driven by an unquenchable need for perfection. The quest for straight

A's became my singular obsession, a measure by which I gauged my worth. Though armed with knowledge, my insecurity tethered me from participation in class, a whisper of doubt cautioning me against the prospect of being wrong.

As the years progressed, my intensity spilled over into my family life, and I was always asking for their assistance to help me study. Discovering I had a photographic memory, I devoured textbooks and visualized notes, creating a mental recall during tests. Flourishing in my academics took its toll on my physical well-being in the form of a stomach ulcer at the age of sixteen.

Despite the physical toll, I achieved what I had been striving for straight A's and salutatorian of my graduating class. My teenage years, fraught with uncertainties and insecurities, found stability within the realm of academic achievement. I weathered the storms of adolescence, emerging on the other side with a list of accomplishments but bearing the scars of an internal struggle that my value was found in those achievements. My new belief was that my grades gave me worth, and I had to be perfect.

After bidding farewell to the familiar halls of high school, I headed to Bible School in Ohio, completing consecutive six-week terms. This marked the inaugural venture away from home. I continued to grapple with the stringent rules dictating my attire. Here, I had to conform and wear the covering. This felt like a new venture but a backward movement on my convictions. I was still plagued with insecurities about my weight. A shyness still clung to me like a shadow, accompanied by the companion of perfectionism. My focus again gravitated toward academic excellence. Despite my shyness, I developed friendships with my roommates and others on my dorm floor. My understanding of the Holy Spirit deepened. The revelation of the unseen forces in the world shattered the sheltered cocoon of my upbringing.

During this time, a Child Development class assignment was to recall an event in my childhood that impacted me. For the first time, I found the courage to articulate on paper the experience in kindergarten-the words that had both wounded and shaped my early self. As I typed the words onto paper, I found myself pausing to reflect deeply. My thoughts wandered to the little boy whose single phrase had such a profound impact on my attitude toward life and myself. I couldn't help but wonder what his reaction would be if he knew the extent of the hurt and the influence his words had.

At the tender age of 19, I penned in my paper a declaration: it was time to release the grip of those painful memories. I recognized the necessity of overcoming the bitterness I harbored towards that little boy, understanding that it was imperative for my own growth and future.

At the end of my assignment, I addressed him directly, stating, "Mike, I forgive you. My life has been very difficult because of you. But I know that in the long run, it was beneficial to me as a person. I know that I am now able to try and be the person that God wants me to be." These reflections served as a catalyst: it helped in releasing the burden of those words and enabled me to perceive myself through the lens of God's perspective rather than the viewpoint of the little boy. This led me into a deeper, more tangible, and authentic relationship with God.

One of my roommates at Bible School, a sweet Canadian girl, spoke often about her cute cousin. Through her connection, I met the love of my life, Brad, a Canadian, hockey-loving farmer. Our romance unfolded across the miles for almost three years until Brad made the courageous move to Indiana. In 1994, we exchanged vows. Brad and I had crafted a clear plan for our future. We would spend two years in Indiana before relocating to Manitoba, where he would join his brother and father on the family farm.

Venturing into our second year of marriage, we heard the call to missions. During the early part of our term, we engaged in discipleship training sessions in Columbus, Ohio, before journeying to Phoenix, Arizona, where we dedicated our time to working with inner-city youth. Those months proved profoundly influential as I deepened my comprehension of God and unearthed insights into my own identity, realizing how my childhood experiences had shaped my approach to life. Brad and I developed a profound affection for the Phoenix area, prompting contemplation about a potential relocation to the city. However, after extension discussion and prayer, we felt God leading us back to Indiana.

Settling back in the family business after missions, Brad and I found a rhythm in marriage and community life. The addition of our first dog, Cronin Walker, a spirited Boston Terrier puppy, and the prospect of purchasing our first truck infused our days with anticipation. My parents decided to venture out on a brief fall vacation to Branson, Missouri. Before leaving, my father made an uncharacteristic visit to my office, engaging in a lighthearted conversation about our decision to buy a truck. That casual exchange became a cherished memory, as it would be our final conversation and the last time I saw him.

Early in the morning on Friday, September 20th, my mom called, "Dad was admitted last night because of chest pains. I told him since we are on vacation, let's not take any chances. They kept him overnight for observation. All the tests have come back okay, and he will be released from the hospital around noon today." Relieved with this news, I headed off to work. Around noon, the phone rang. The secretary told me that my mom was on the phone. I picked it up, "Lisa, Dad is in code blue. They are trying to revive him. I'll call back as soon as I know anything." Shock, unbelief, and confusion overwhelmed me. I needed a place to process, and I retreated into the tiny restroom. "God, save my dad," I cried out. An indescribable peace enveloped me. Moments later, the devastating news arrived – my father was gone.

The ensuing hours unfolded in a haze, guided only by God's grace and the gift of shock. Friends helped us navigate airline flight arrangements. Before we headed to the airport, friends gathered in our living room, and as we circled around in prayer, I collapsed onto the floor in tears as the reality of losing my father sank in.

With Brad by my side, we boarded a plane to meet my brother Nate, and together we flew to a small airport in Springfield, Missouri to meet our grieving mother. Upon arriving late in the evening, we considered a motel stay, but mom just wanted to be home. My mom knew that sleep would elude her, so she took the wheel and drove the entire 600 miles back to Indiana. The blackness of the night reflected the heavy spirit of shock and grief that filled the car. Unrecognized grief became my friend.

A month prior to my father's death, he had convened the entire family. He told us his intention was to sell the family business: a construction company and lumberyard, that he had started with his brothers in the 1960s unless my brother and I expressed interest. Seated in a dimly lit back corner around a circular table of a restaurant in Brown County, Indiana, I told my father, "Brad and I plan to move to Manitoba next year. This summer, we started drafting the paperwork." Expressing my genuine excitement, I added, "I'm thrilled that you have a buyer, allowing you to semi-retire, and you and Mom can get involved in mission work." My brother, too, affirmed his commitment to staying in Louisville, offering his blessing for the businesses to be sold.

With my father's sudden departure, the potential buyer withdrew, and the future of the business became uncertain. Witnessing my mother's grief, compounded by her ongoing role as the primary caregiver for her sister Joanna, the responsibilities ahead felt overwhelming. Given my administrative role in the business, I helped navigate the necessary changes needed in the business to cover the enormous void left by my father. I soon realized that my promise to Brad, and the prospect of moving to Manitoba, was not going to happen.

Life's twists and turns over the years had etched in me the belief that I was not enough, fearful, different, and judged. I carried labels of perfectionist, rebel, and rule follower, which created the framework through which I viewed life. I found it challenging to love myself. Consequently, I grappled with understanding and fully embracing God's love for me.

The profound loss of my father, coupled with the responsibility of managing the family business and the pressure to step into a quasi-husband role for my mother, intensified this framework. To cope, I subconsciously adopted a defensive stance, concealing my genuine emotions to survive. Strength became my refuge, and I believed my worth was now tied to my ability to provide and fulfill responsibilities. The prevailing sentiments were that my emotions were best buried and forgotten, and I bore the weight of having to manage it all on my own.

On the surface, everything was fine - I was happy and content, actively engaged in church, work, and social activities. Brad and I had been married for almost three years when we began conversations about starting a family. Since childhood, I always dreamed of becoming a mother. Despite being overwhelmed with responsibilities and feeling confident in the foundation of our relationship, we were ready to embark on to the next chapter of our lives. Several months later, with anticipation tingling in the air, we eagerly awaited the results of the pregnancy test. As we sat together, gazing at the blue double lines, a wave of excitement washed over us.

CHAPTER 2

The Defining Moment

There are two ways to live your life. One is though nothing is a miracle. The other is as though everything is a miracle.
Albert Einstein[2]

I gently tapped Brad's shoulder and attempted to rouse him from his sleep. "Brad, my contractions are getting more intense. I think it's time to head to the hospital, " I whispered. In a groggy state, Brad rolled out of bed, the sun not yet up. It was ten days past my due date. Grabbing the overnight bag I had prepared for this moment; we drove to the hospital. The tension of this moment could be felt. Brad and I, filled with anticipation and anxiety, entered the hospital through the ER entrance, making our way to the third floor.

To our disappointment, after an examination, the medical staff informed me that our baby wasn't quite ready for arrival and suggested we walk around a nearby store for a few hours. Reluctantly, we followed their advice, choosing the local Walmart. Determined to progress the labor, I navigated the aisles, occasionally pausing as light contractions stole my breath, and I clutched the shopping cart to steady myself. Periodic breaks were necessary to ease the pressure on my lower back. The time stretched, feeling long and exhausting, but eventually, a sense of readiness settled in, and I believed the time for our baby's arrival had finally come.

After enduring a strenuously long labor involving hours of pushing and the use of forceps, my baby's heartbeat began to weaken. It became evident that an emergency C-section was necessary. Nurses whisked me away, and I was rendered unconscious. The next thing I remember is waking up, my mind hazy and feeling immediate pain. I looked around the large room, with hanging curtains as dividers. I was in the recovery room. As I tried to gather my bearings, I immediately felt panic. *Was my baby ok? Where was my baby?* Thankfully, Brad was sitting beside my bed.

Focusing my gaze on him, I anxiously asked about our little one's well-being. He delivered the news that we had a baby boy, and he was doing good! What a relief! I wanted to see my boy! Two hours later, I was finally cleared to leave the recovery room. Brad pushed me into my room as my little bundle arrived in his bassinet, swaddled in the standard hospital blanket adorned with blue and pink stripes from the hospital nursery. Overwhelmed with immediate love, connection, and joy, the sight of my beautiful little boy, Bryson Kordell, brought relief, and I eagerly waited to hold him in my arms.

Bryson made his entrance into the world during the early morning hours, leaving both of us sleep-deprived. As the soft hues of sunrise bathed the room after spending several hours together as a family of three, we began sharing the exciting news with family and friends. The day unfolded with a stream of loved ones arriving to catch a glimpse of our precious son. Along with their visits, they brought thoughtful gifts, flower arrangements, teddy bears, and a plush little white sheep. Because of the C-section, I found myself in a groggy state and experiencing considerable pain. As the day ended, Brad and I opted for

Bryson to stay in the nursery overnight, providing me an opportunity to secure as much rest as possible.

Choosing to return home for a restful night, Brad arrived back by my bedside early the next morning as I was struggling to rouse myself from sleep. The night had been rough, awakening every couple of hours to administer pain medication. My body throbbed with discomfort from surgery. Throughout the restless night, my mind swirled with reflections on the events of the past 24 hours. I had officially become a mother.

Brad sat quietly beside my bed, holding my hand. The lavender walls left a soothing hue. My heart was happy, but my body hurt. I was grateful that I had chosen to have Bryson be in the nursery for the night, but I was ready to have him with me again.

Shortly before the shift change in the morning, the night nurse entered our room. Bryson was not with her. She quietly came over to my bedside and said, "During Bryson's stay in the nursery, the nurse noticed troubling signs – a jerking left arm and twitching left eye that resembled a seizure." She went on to say that the doctor wanted to do more tests. Brad and I sat in silence. Confusion, fear, and questions flashed into our heads. My first words were, "Can we see him?" The nurse kindly replied, "Yes, but it will need to be soon because he will be taken to get a CT scan done." I had barely been out of bed since my c-section, but I wanted to see my son. Before the nurse left the room, she asked us, "Do you want to see a priest or pastor?" We were taken aback. Is it really that bad? Was my son going to die? Fear exploded in my mind; tears fell. We told her no, we didn't need one, and our minds struggled to think. We wanted to call our family and friends again, but who to call and what do we tell them? We didn't know anything except that fear had entered the room.

With assistance from Brad, I carefully rose from bed, and he helped me put on my blue and white plaid nightgown I had brought from home. Slowly, he wheeled me down the seemingly long hall to the nursery. Turning the corner past the nurse's desk, the doors to the nursery came into view. Anticipation heightened; Bryson's little bassinet stood just inside the door to the right. Stepping out of the wheelchair, I walked over. Though Bryson looked the same as when he left for the nursery, everything had changed. He was wrapped in a teddy bear blanket covered with stars. We asked if we could hold him. With the nurse's approval, Brad gently lifted him out and placed him in my arms. As we gazed down at our son in a mix of wonder and disbelief, the magnitude of the moment hit us. He was beautiful, and he was ours. For about ten minutes, we stood there, whispering words of love, courage, and peace over him-words that, in many ways, were directed to our aching hearts. Brad offered a prayer for Bryson as I reluctantly returned him to his bassinet. An unsettling thought crossed my mind: *Will I get to hold my son again?* Tearfully, Brad wheeled me back to our room, where the nurse reassured us that the CT scan would soon be conducted, and the doctor would provide us with information on what was happening.

As we sat alone in the room, in a state of shock, we called our family and friends to share the unfolding situation. We advised them to hold off on visiting until we had more information. By mid-morning, our doctor arrived and conveyed the results of the CT scan-a blood clot in Bryson's left artery. He explained that the hospital lacked the necessary resources for this critical condition and that a transfer to Riley's Children's Hospital in Indianapolis, a three-hour drive from home, was imperative.

My physical pain was secondary to everything else. Critical decisions loomed, with a short timeframe for resolution. Originally, the plan was for me to be in the hospital for at least three days due to the c-section. However, it was only 36 hours later. Would the hospital permit my early release to be with my son? How soon would the ambulance arrive from Indy for his transport? Calls were made to friends and family, with Brad shouldering the bulk of the calls, recounting the story repeatedly: "Our son had a seizure, they found a blood clot, he is getting ready to be transferred to Riley." Hearing those words, the surreal nature of the situation hit me. *Was this a dream? Was this really happening to us?*

We had recently changed churches, and we reached out to both the pastor who officiated our wedding and the new pastor we were getting to know. They graciously joined us, offering prayers and support. My mother and other family members soon arrived, providing a much-needed presence. Brad, unfortunately, couldn't have his family physically there, as they resided in Manitoba, Canada, but their prayers reached us. Close friends gathered to lend their support and prayers. My best friend Fran and her husband Merv wanted to travel with us to Indianapolis, even though her own due date was merely four days away. After heartfelt discussions, Merv managed to convince her that it wasn't the wisest course of action. Fran grappled with this decision but ultimately chose to stay behind. Lavon and his wife Carol, close friends from church, offered words of understanding and comfort. They had experienced hospital stays and the heartbreaking loss of two daughters. Despite their reassurances, a lingering fear persisted in my mind. *Will Bryson die too?*

The hospital granted permission for me to accompany Bryson to Riley, and Brad rushed home to gather clothes for our hospital stay. When the ambulance finally arrived, we had a brief moment to say goodbye to Bryson. After the CT scan, he was connected to various monitors to check his vitals. Seeing him so small and alone- and knowing we couldn't accompany him in the ambulance, leaving him with strangers, tears fell. The unknown weighed heavy, and questions rolled through our heads. *How long will we be there? Will we see Bryson alive again?* I didn't want these thoughts. Shock and fear had invaded my mind.

The day was cold and gloomy, a typical January day in northern Indiana. The nurses helped me get into our Chevy Grand Prix. My body hurt. I was given pain meds to take along, but my body was still in the recovery stage. Driving in a car for three hours wasn't going to help. Brad placed pillows on each side of me, covering me with a blanket. Our friends, Lavon and Carol, volunteered to escort us to Indianapolis and with them leading the way, we headed off to follow our son into the unknown of what lay ahead.

When we arrived at Riley, we were told that Bryson was in the Neonatal Intensive Care Unit (NICU). My physical pain was high after the car ride, but my anxiousness to see my son drove me. The hospital hallway stretched ahead, the sterile white walls reflecting the harsh fluorescence of overhead lights. We walked slowly, numbly riding the elevator up several floors and down another sterile white hall to the ICU unit. Upon arrival, we received instructions to wash our hands and don the required gowns before entering. After we awkwardly navigated the process of putting on the light blue paper gowns, we were finally ready. We located Bryson among six other babies, positioned at the back of the room. I gently reached out to touch my precious little boy.

Since we arrived in the early evening, no tests were conducted on the first night, leaving us in anticipation of what the morning would bring. We were grateful for the offerings of Riley hospital, as we were accommodated at the nearby Ronald McDonald house. With the limitations of being in Bryson's room for only a few hours at a time, having a retreat was a welcome relief.

The following morning, as we entered the room, the nurse was attaching electrodes to Bryson's head for his first EEG. He lay there peacefully and snuggled tight in his blanket, unaffected by the procedure, while my heart ached in pain. As I sat in a rocking chair close to Bryson, my eyes scanned the room, and once again, fear and disbelief gripped me. Seeing the other babies lying in their incubators, I realized I wasn't alone in navigating this challenging situation, yet the road felt desolate and difficult, and the weight pressed heavily on my heart.

Finally, during our afternoon visit to see Bryson, the doctor arrived with information. Their specialist had thoroughly examined the CT scan and EEG, revealing that Bryson had suffered a stroke.

The revelation was devastating, babies aren't supposed to have strokes! While the news was heart-wrenching, it provided some clarity. Though his prognosis remained uncertain, the diagnosis did not indicate any threats to his life. Immediately, he was prescribed Phenobarbital for his seizures. The nurses arrived bearing a folder filled with numerous pamphlets and information about the state's First Steps therapy program.

The abundance of information we needed to absorb was overwhelming. We carefully fed Bryson his bottle of formula, holding him close for the few hours we could be with him. In those moments, we focused on his rhythmic breathing, his dark hair, his soft skin. He was beautiful! The prayers from our family and friends enveloped us, and we sensed the presence of our Almighty God.

As we ambled back to the Ronald McDonald house, my body screamed in protest, and my mind yearned to escape. All I wanted was to crawl into bed, hoping to wake up and discover this was all a dream. I felt like a zombie, unable to navigate the onslaught of physical and emotional pain. Climbing a short, wide flight of stairs on the way to our room, I clung to the wall railing and pulled myself up in agony. I told myself I had to be strong for my son. In the solitude of our room, I sank into the bathtub and cried out to God. "God, where are you, WHY? It isn't supposed to be this way."

After spending four days at Riley, we finally placed Bryson into his new car seat when he was six days old, ready to embark on the journey back home. Finally, we were a family of three, free from the constant presence of nurses or doctors. We were determined to provide Bryson with every opportunity to live his best life. Although we returned home with Bryson on seizure medication, we prayed fervently that he would not suffer any side effects from the stroke. Upon our return, we joyously recorded his first diaper change, his first bottle, and his first bath at home, reassuring ourselves that everyone was going to be okay.

Defining Moments can *break* you, but trust God to let them *make* you.

The shock was a gift from God. It acted as a protective covering, providing a respite from the harsh reality life has thrown us. At 26 years old, I navigated the uncharted waters of motherhood with my firstborn, Bryson. Denial became my newfound companion after the initial shock subsided. "Babies, just sleep, poop, and eat anyway," I reasoned. Bryson seemed -and acted- normal in my eyes. Administering liquid medication became a routine, it blended seamlessly into our daily lives. At six weeks old, Bryson underwent evaluation by the First Steps program, followed by his initial physical therapy appointment a few days later. These were the only visible reminders of the diagnosis that we received when Bryson was two days old.

Bryson, for the most part, was a quiet and content baby. Yet, there were moments of inconsolable crying that we attributed to colic-just another facet of normal babyhood. Family from Manitoba, including Brad's parents and sisters, visited. My mother frequently lent a helping hand. We ventured out to see friends. We dressed him in adorable outfits, and we took pictures of him with our Boston Terrier, Cronin. His smiles were frequent. In the first six months of his life, we took him on his first airplane ride across the country. We embarked on a 1100-mile road trip to Manitoba to introduce him to the rest of Brad's family. Bryson attended his uncle and aunt's wedding on the Belle of Louisville and gracefully floated down the Ohio River. We were a family; engaged in all the *normal* activities, we believed everything would be okay.

But the undercurrent of grief was lurking. Brad and I struggled to label it, uncertain of how to confront its presence. Our prayers for Bryson's healing were frequent. We openly shared the details of his birth and diagnosis with our church congregation, expressing hope that time would reveal his well-being and complete healing by God. We conveyed gratitude for our healthy little boy whom we loved deeply. Yet, reality painted a different picture as signs emerged that Bryson wasn't using his right arm, consistently keeping his right hand clenched. Despite these cues, we clung to our friend, denial.

CHAPTER 3
Comparison and Denial

You don't have to compare your problems with other people's problems. You don't have to dismiss our feelings by saying "other people have it worse." You are allowed to feel down. You are allowed to grieve no matter what size of your loss.

Jerico Silver[3]

As we embarked on the journey through the early months of Bryson's life, within the familiar confines of our cozy little house, the world seemed to retain its sense of normalcy. Yet, as we ventured beyond the comfort of our home to interact with family and friends, a veil of denial enveloped us. I was reluctant to acknowledge the emotions simmering just beneath the surface, hinting that perhaps life was not unfolding according to my expectations.

During the challenging moments, it was the unwavering presence of my best friend Fran and her husband Merv that provided solace and support during Bryson's birth trauma and the weeks to follow. Our lives had been intricately woven together for countless years, their steadfast companionship a testament to the enduring strength of our bond. However, intertwined in the beauty of our friendship was a connection that stirred my feelings of comparison and denial. This connection demanded acknowledgment as part of our shared story. This is how the story began……

The church sanctuary stood as a sanctuary of peace, bathed in the warm glow of sunlight streaming through the large, stained-glass windows. The wooden benches were worn smooth over the years by devoted members. Each pew held memories of prayers whispered, hymns sung, and moments of peace.

Near the pulpit, a group of young girls played happily. Amidst the playfulness of the young girls, one stood out from the rest. Fran, a thirteen-year-old with an air of shyness, observed the lively scene from a wooden pew near the back. Her chestnut hair, woven into pigtails, hung by her face as she watched with a shy smile. Today marked her family's first time attending this church. By Fran's side stood her mother, Mary Ellen, a woman of gentle demeanor and warm smiles. Grasping Fran's hand, Mary Ellen approached the young girls, "Fran, why don't you go join these sweet girls? They seem to be having so much fun." Fran hesitated for a moment, her eyes flickering from her mother to the energetic group of girls. Encouraged by her mother's gentle nod, she took a tentative step forward.

Caught in the enjoyment of the game Statue, I noticed Fran approaching. The youngest of the group at eleven years old, I understood the feeling of uncertainty. Guided by an instinct that recognized a kindred spirit, I left the game and walked over to Fran. "Hey there, I'm Lisa!" I exclaimed; do you want to join us? We're having so much fun!" Fran, pleasantly surprised by my invitation, couldn't help smiling in return.

As the years unfolded, Fran and my friendship deepened into a lifelong bond, transcending the initial shyness that marked our first meeting in the church sanctuary. The large brick farmhouse, Fran's home, nestled against a backdrop of rolling fields and endless skies, became one of our hangouts. We spent afternoons at the farm, escaping with four-wheelers through the fields to the woods to play. The scent of adventure hung in the air as we navigated through the woods, creating lasting memories.

Summer camps, church campouts, conferences, and softball games were times of laughter, adventuresome moments, and priceless memories. We even meticulously compiled scrapbooks filled with our treasured photographs long before scrapbooking became a trendy hobby. We attended different high schools, and we always enjoyed bantering about which school was best.

One sunny Saturday afternoon, Fran and I decided a trip to Target was necessary. The air was infused with the scent of freshly cut grass and the promise of a day filled with possibilities. It all began innocently as Fran and I entered through the automatic doors, the air conditioning providing a refreshing break from the sun's warmth. Shopping carts in hand, we meandered through the aisles.

Eventually, hands full with shirts and skirts, we headed for the dressing room. Taking turns showing off our new outfits, we exited in and out of the dressing room doors. In an unforeseen twist of events, Fran's dressing room door, seemingly secure in its frame, betrayed its hinges and, with an audible creak, crashed onto Fran's dainty little toe. The initial moment froze in time as I heard Fran's sharp scream cut through the air. Bursting out of my dressing room, I grabbed the dressing room door, looking down as a vivid hue of red began to pool around Fran's injured toe, the color stark against the sterile, white tiles.

A store associate rushed to the scene, eyes wide with concern, her walkie-talkie cracking with conversations as she asked for assistance. Another employee hurriedly fetched a first aid kit, attempting to address the situation. With Fran's pain showing no signs of lessening, we quickly realized the necessity of seeking professional medical attention. Fran and I thanked the store associate, who had responded promptly, and without further delay, we slowly walked to the exit, Fran leaning heavily on me, limping, and wincing in pain.

As we approached Fran's Ford Mercury, a manual, I suddenly realized that I had to drive, and I had never driven a stick shift before. Fran, amid her pain, let out a chuckle. She knew this experience was going to be a memorable one. I slid into the driver's seat, and my fingers wrapped around the gear stick. The air inside the car was thick with a blend of Fran's pain and my nervousness. The moment of truth arrived, and with a careful hand, I engaged the first gear. The stick shift resisted at first, but with a gentle nudge, it settled into place. The car began to inch forward and then stalled. This occurred several times before I mastered the coordination of the clutch, gas pedal, and stick shift dance. Thankfully, we made it to the closest urgent care without any issues. They wrapped up her foot and gave her a prescription for an antibiotic and pain medication. I helped her hobble to the car, and I slowly navigated our way home, taking as many back roads as possible. To this day, I have never driven a stick shift again. The memories of that day still seared in my mind.

Fran and I were the dynamic duo at the forefront of our church youth group, perpetually brainstorming the next exciting event to organize. Our social circle expanded when my brother Nate and his best friend Merv joined forces with us, forming an inseparable foursome. From hanging out at Burger King, movie nights, and softball games to spontaneous road trips, we shared countless moments of laughter and camaraderie.

Although Merv and I once dared to test the waters of a romantic connection with a movie date, it quickly became evident that our bond was meant to remain firmly rooted in friendship. Divine intervention, however, had other plans as sparks ignited between Fran and Merv, leading them down the path of marriage.

When I introduced Brad to Fran as my boyfriend, she made a surprising revelation - she had crossed paths with him during her days at Bible school, even possessing a photo of Brad wearing her shirt from a themed event. It added another layer of connection to our already intertwined lives.

Eight and a half months prior to our own wedding, Fran and Merv exchanged vows. As we embraced the adventure of marriage, our husbands seamlessly integrated into our tight-knit circle, solidifying our bond even further.

Together, we embarked on unforgettable vacations, seamlessly blending new memories with cherished old ones. We both decided to leave the church of Fran, and my upbringing and we ventured together into a new congregation, reaffirming the enduring strength of our friendship through life's ever-changing landscapes.

It was a hot and humid August day in Indiana. With the door to my office firmly shut, I aimed to create a haven of concentration, shielding myself from the possible interruptions of fellow employees. Since the age of sixteen, I'd been involved in a myriad of roles within my family's construction company and lumberyard. On this day, I was fully immersed in scrutinizing the monthly financial statements. Amidst the scorching heat outside, my office was enveloped in a brisk chill coming from the air conditioning vent. The breeze sent shivers down my spine as I focused on the pressing task before me.

As I reviewed the paperwork, there came a knock at my door. Glancing up from my desk, I was met with the cheerful sight of my closest friend, Fran, looking into the window of my door. She worked just up the road at a nearby factory and occasionally swung by after her shift. Today, though, there was something in her demeanor that was different, something bubbling beneath the surface.

"Lisa, I've got something to tell you: I'm pregnant!" Fran blurted out with a sparkle in her eye, her excitement palpable. A moment of astonishment hung in the air before I leaped to my feet, eager to celebrate her news. I wrapped my arms around her in a warm, congratulatory hug. I whispered softly in her ear, "I'm pregnant too!"

We each took a step back, a shared sense of excitement coursing between us. Fran quickly grabbed me in a hug again, and we soaked in the news together. In all our conversations, the notion of us becoming pregnant simultaneously had never crossed our minds.

In the best friend manner, we chatted animatedly about our respective journeys, when we'd found out, our due dates, and our chosen doctors. After a few minutes, I gently interrupted, saying, "Fran, you can't share this with anyone just yet. Brad and I have not told anyone. You're the first to know." Fran chuckled, feeling truly honored to be the keeper of our shared secret. As she rose to depart, I realized the time had come to share this wonderful news with my mom and other close family members. The important paperwork could wait until tomorrow. Today, I had thrilling news to share.

Sharing the experience of a first-time pregnancy was the icing on the cake for our friendship. The journey was a delightful whirlwind as we excitedly prepared for the arrival of our little ones. Our pregnancies not only magnified the contrasts in Fran's and my physical appearance but also brought out our unique charm. Fran, with her tall and slender frame, stood in stark contrast to my petite and, to put it kindly, "plump" stature, a feature that had been a source of my low self-esteem since my kindergarten years. Yet, I took this opportunity to not concern myself with my weight. I joyfully gained an extra 50 pounds. As the due dates for our babies drew nearer, Fran and I decided to hold a joint baby shower. It was fun to share the excitement together with our family and friends. Our due dates were just two weeks apart.

Comparison and Denial

Bryson delayed his appearance and arrived 10 days late. Miranda, their daughter, arrived precisely on her due date, just four days after Bryson was born, while we were still in Indianapolis. Just as Fran had wrestled with not being able to come to be with us, my heart broke that I could not celebrate with Fran on the arrival of her sweet one.

Fran and I would talk daily about our sweet babies. Bryson and Miranda got to meet each other the day after we returned home. Their meeting was precious. We told them all about all the fun adventures they were going to have together. I pushed aside the nagging in my head about Bryson's uncertain future and believed that he was going to be totally fine.

Brad and I were aware that Bryson might face challenges, but we didn't know the extent. As first-time parents, we were uncertain about what to expect and when to expect it. I read books about child development, but as they all say, every child develops at their own pace. Eventually, Fran started talking about the milestones Miranda was achieving – rolling over, sitting up, crawling, walking and the list goes on. I had purchased a "Baby's First Year" calendar and all the bright and cheerful stickers that came with it to put on the day of each of the firsts. This calendar stayed blank. I had a white, ordinary binder with monthly calendar pages where I kept records of blood draws, PT, OT, ST appointments, hospitalizations, illnesses, medications, and doctor appointments, none of which had happy, colorful stickers. These were marred with sadness.

Do not compare your trials with anyone else. Do not minimize your pain, your heartache.

This poem below, published in most books regarding special needs, found its way into my world. It became my anthem, the truth of the words, a powerful and an accurate description of my life.

Welcome to Holland by Emily Perl Kingsley[4]

When you're going to have a baby, it's like planning a fabulous vacation trip - to Italy. You buy a bunch of guidebooks and make your wonderful plans. The Coliseum. The Michelangelo David. The gondolas in Venice. You may learn some handy phrases in Italian. It's all very exciting.

After months of eager anticipation, the day finally arrives. You pack your bags and off you go. Several hours later, the plane lands. The stewardess comes in and says, "Welcome to Holland." "Holland?!?" you say. "What do you mean Holland?? I signed up for Italy! I'm supposed to be in Italy. All my life I've dreamed of going to Italy." But there's been a change in the flight plan. They've landed in Holland and there you must stay.

The important thing is that they haven't taken you to a horrible, disgusting, filthy place, full of pestilence, famine, and disease. It's just a different place. So, you must go out and buy new guidebooks. And you must learn a whole new language. And you will meet a whole new group of people you would never have met. It's just a different place. It's slower paced than Italy, less flashy than Italy.

But after you've been there for a while and you catch your breath, you look around.... and you begin to notice that Holland has windmills....and Holland has tulips. Holland even has Rembrandts. But everyone you know is busy coming and going from Italy... and they're all bragging about what a wonderful time they had there. And for the rest of your life, you will say "Yes, that's where I was supposed to go. That's what I had planned." And the pain of that will never, ever, ever, ever go away... because the loss of that dream is a very significant loss. But... if you spend your life mourning the fact that you didn't get to Italy, you may never be free to enjoy the very special, the very lovely things ... about Holland.

With our precious newborns in our arms, Fran and I stood at the threshold of the next chapter of motherhood. Referencing the poem, Fran and I both left the airport at the same time. Fran arrived in Italy as planned, but as I claimed the words to this poem, my heart could not fully embrace the truth that I had landed in Holland. I knew I was there, but I didn't want to voice it aloud- acknowledge the truth- because accepting it would make it all true.

I unintentionally suppressed my emotions, left the airport in Holland, and embarked on a relentless journey filled with busyness. Outwardly, I invested every ounce of effort into ensuring my son's success, all while diminishing the turbulence of my inner turmoil: denial, doubt, confusion, and fear. I compared my trials to those around me, a voice within me declaring, *"Be strong. This is nothing compared to what other people are going through."* Much like the coping mechanisms of my childhood, I pushed these emotions deep down, a subconscious act aimed at avoiding my harsh reality.

I hesitated to confront the painful truth: the prayer I had whispered to God, "Anything but a handicapped child," seemed unheard. An evil voice also gnawed at my soul, whispering, "God heard you; He doesn't care about you." My battle for faith, trust, and hope raged.

> **"We're not necessarily doubting that God will do the best for us; we are wondering how painful the best will turn out to be." C.S. Lewis[5]**

The chill of the winter night clung relentlessly in the air, seeping through the cracks of our small yet cozy home. The walls, adorned with an array of family photographs capturing moments frozen in time, seemed to close in around me as I tiptoed across the hallway to Bryson's room. I gently pulled a pale quilted blanket adorned with sheep to Bryson's neck. A creation of love from my mother, Wilma, I tuck the quilt and trace every delicate curve and contour of my precious little boy. His chest rose and fell with a rhythmic cadence of innocence, a tiny symphony of breaths that spoke of a world untouched by worries. Wiping a lone tear from my eye, I allowed the weight of worry to settle on my shoulders. Seeking refuge, I made my way to the home office. The office, bathed in the soft glow of the desk lamp, invited me in. I reached for my Bible, a precious treasure. Its pages infused with wisdom and solace, beckoned me to seek refuge within its sacred verses. Seated in contemplative silence, I opened to the Book of Job. Each word became a plea for understanding and guidance for navigating the uncharted roads that lay ahead. My mind wrestling with questions, drawing parallels to Job's trials and tribulations. Was I strong enough to face my own challenges with the same resilience?

The sacred space of my home office bore witness that night to my silent pleas. I sought not only answers, but more importantly, the strength to navigate the challenges that lay ahead.

The frigid winter wind lashed at my jacket as I approached the welcoming haven of the church. Stepping through the wide window-clad doors, the biting cold relinquished its grip and gave way to the warm embrace of the foyer. The air inside hummed with a comforting familiarity, the sound of friendly chatter and laughter.

Despite the external warmth, an internal storm raged within me. Denial, doubt, and fear continued their battle for my soul, and I felt like a lone soldier on the losing end. Noticing a friend near the coffee bar, I approached her and sought solace in a hug. Little did I know that this embrace would release a flood of words regarding my struggles with Bryson.

Words spilled out, and as she placed her hand on my arm, she responded, "Be grateful for what you have; you could be in Haiti." Those words, born from her own perspective, stung, their impact echoing the devastation of the recent earthquake in Haiti. Taken aback, I managed to finish the conversation, and with a fog settling over my thoughts, I entered the sanctuary.

I was oblivious to the worship and sermon, my mind spinning with thoughts, "Lisa, see just what I was telling you, be strong, it could be worse, God is here… just try harder, just believe, He will provide." The truth, God will provide, was accurate but the other words I told myself were lies that I had believed for way too long.

I wrestled with conflicting emotions throughout the day, torn with thoughts of "be strong" and "I can't do this." By the evening, anger simmered beneath the surface, and seeking refuge, I retreated to my desk. There in the quiet of the evening, I poured out my thoughts onto paper. Buried emotions, fears, and doubts flowed, a torrent of raw honesty. I told God I was tired, exhausted, and that my life felt like it had experienced an earthquake of its own.

I sought neither to downplay my heartache nor to diminish its significance; rather, I yearned for someone who would genuinely care for and acknowledge the depth of my pain. God met me in that sacred space. The ink on the paper became a place of His divine grace and mercy. What started as a venting of my anger and fear transformed into a place where God spoke:

"Lisa, stop comparing the road I have you on with other people's roads. I give each one of you a unique journey to travel, and with each earthquake, I will provide. I will help you dig. I AM the strong steel that will not let it crush you and bury you!! I am here to give you life and give it to you abundantly!! I am here to hold your hand and to carry the shovel when you are tired!! You are MY child, I love you, just let go!! Yes, I have given you a special needs child for a reason. I know you were the perfect mother for Bryson. And because I gave him to you, I will help you. Stop worrying, let go of control, let go of the fears. March ahead with ME. Yes, I have big plans for you that go beyond the realm of a special needs child, but I plan to use that platform. I plan to use moments like this to have you reach others who are crushed and buried with their own earthquakes. Lisa, rise up out of the rubble and run to me. I will bandage the wounds.

I will ease the pain!! Stop looking at this road as too long and dirty! I am there with you to help you pave it into a smooth and joyful road! Come my child, come, and rest in ME!!! Love God"

This was the solace I craved. His words acted as a soothing balm for my weary soul. In that moment, tears flowed, and I sensed that He cared and knew the depth of my pain. He would provide. Yet, I struggled to fully grasp all the truth He had shared. While my mind acknowledged the reality, my heart still needed healing.

CHAPTER 4
All Things Medical and Therapy

> To wait with openness and trust is an enormously radical attitude toward life. It is giving up control over our future and letting God define our life.
> Henri Nouwen[6]

In a dusty corner of Bryson's room, nestled among the shelves, I found the ordinary white binder. Its unassuming exterior paid no tribute to the weight of the memories written within the pages, a testament to the journey that I traveled beginning in 1998 with Bryson's arrival into the world. Within its pages was a chronicle of the first three tumultuous years. Each entry represented the resilience and endurance of a little boy, my son, who faced more than his fair share of challenges.

As Bryson approached seven months, Brad and I engaged in a discussion about the prospect of discontinuing his seizure medication.

We reached out to Bryson's pediatrician, who connected us with a local neurologist. The referral led us to a neurologist in South Bend, approximately an hour drive from our house. Following the completion of all necessary medical paperwork, I received a call from the office scheduling a sleep deprived EEG and an MRI.

Keeping a 7-month-old baby awake for an extended period of time proved to be a challenging task, and the struggle extended to keeping ourselves alert. The goal was to ensure Bryson was sufficiently drowsy so that once the wires were attached to his head, he would drift off to sleep, allowing for an accurate test. With the EEG and MRI completed, we waited for the much-anticipated doctor's appointment.

Pulling into the parking lot, Brad parked beside a row of shrubs marking the edge of a neatly trimmed lawn. The landscape cast a calming atmosphere, so different from the inner ramblings of my mind. The building, modest in size, featured a neutral palette, a combination of soft beige and light gray. Large windows flanked the double entrance doors. I approached the reception desk as Brad carried Bryson over to the comfortable chairs positioned under the large windows.

We soon found ourselves in a large, stark white exam room. The neurologist, clad in a well-tailored shirt with suspenders, entered with an air of arrogance. He immediately revealed the results of the EEG and MRI. His demeanor was pretentious, evident in the way he delivered the news. "Bryson's EEG revealed numerous epileptic spikes in his brain, and the MRI showed that your son's left-brain hemisphere is 76% dead!" Without a sense of kindness, the words crushed us in dismay. The adage "sticks and stones may break my bones, but words will never hurt me" proved false; those words stung deeply. Our hopeful expectations for the appointment were shattered, thrusting us out of denial into a painful reality. It launched us into a place that we didn't want to go. The healing hadn't happened yet. God, why? At that moment, I made an inner vow – *I was going to be strong and do everything within my power for my child.*

Amidst the turmoil of those words, one positive point emerged from this appointment. The doctor clarified that the stroke had occurred 3-6 weeks before Bryson was born. This revelation brought some relief, as I had been struggling with anger towards the doctors involved in his delivery. I had pondered what could have been done differently, if only they had intervened sooner, or I hadn't pushed so long. I was able to put that anger aside, but the thoughts then reflected on me.

Shortly after learning about the timing of Bryson's stroke, sleep eluded me, and I found myself consumed with swirling thoughts. What had I done during pregnancy that might have impacted his left carotid artery, leading to the blood clot? The weighty sensation in the pit of my stomach mirrored the turmoil in my mind. I revisited various events and scenarios, seeking answers, but found only increasing despair. As I stared up at the ceiling, I wished fervently that the blame was on the doctor, for the burden of knowing I might have played a role felt unbearable. In the silence of the night, I lifted my prayers to God, confessing my guilt and the heavy burden of blame I carried. In that moment, I felt a calming presence wash over me, and eventually, I drifted off into an uneasy sleep.

In the weeks that followed, such nights became a recurring ordeal. There was no quick fix for the weight of blame that gripped me relentlessly. The exhaustion from caring for Bryson, coupled with this internal struggle, became overwhelming. Yet, I realized I couldn't remain trapped in this cycle of guilt. I needed to release these thoughts and trust that God held the answers. One evening as I rocked Bryson to sleep, my heart weighed down by the burden of guilt, I looked into his innocent eyes and knew that it was time to let go. Silently, I prayed for God's help in releasing the blame. In that moment, I felt a profound sense of peace wash over me, understanding that dwelling on the past wouldn't change anything. What mattered the most was how I moved forward, advocating for the best possible future for my son. With a deep breath, I surrendered the weight of blame to God, trusting in His guidance.

My mother and I entered through the main entrance of the hospital. I carried Bryson in his car seat, and we walked through the labyrinth of hallways to reach the lab, located across from the emergency room. Seizures, an unwelcome companion since birth, demand a regular and unwavering ritual – the dreaded blood draws. My heart felt heavy with sadness as I knew what was ahead of us. The receptionist knew us by name, and soon we entered the small room. Dim, gentle lighting provided a softness against the harsh white walls. Against the back wall was the examination table, which I slowly approached. I removed Bryson from his car seat and held him close to my chest as I waited for the phlebotomist, a medical professional trained in blood draws, to enter. My mother settled into the hard, black chair in the corner, her presence a steadfast pillar of support. I heard a gentle knock on the door, and Mary entered the room. I immediately felt a moment of relief as she was my favorite. I gently laid Bryson down on the unyielding white surface of the table, and my hand rested on his chest as I waited.

The act of holding him still during these painful procedures was a familiar, heart-wrenching, routine. His veins, small and elusive, were inherited from his mother and grandmother. Mary's gentle touch and understanding eyes softens the momentary pain inflicted on Bryson. She, too, despised her role as the one causing his discomfort. As his cries echoed through the room and the needle pierced his delicate skin, Mary and I engaged in casual chatter.

Immediately after the correct amount of blood was drawn, I picked up Bryson. His face was flushed and his eyes slightly swollen as he continued to cry. Bringing him close, I rocked and soothed his weary body. My mom, tears in her eyes, approached me and took Bryson. As he finally settled down, she placed him in his car seat.

Those moments I was grateful for my mom's strength. She shared the emotional turbulence of the blood draws.

The calendar page for the month of April 1999, in that seemingly white ordinary binder, was full of my handwriting as I scribbled every day. Each event cast a shadow of the challenges that tested both the resilience of my spirit and the endurance of Bryson's tiny frame. The month was marked by a surge in seizure activity and the onset of various illnesses, thrusting us into a disheartening routine of hospital visits for chest x-rays, pediatrician consultations for medication, and urgent care trips during late-night fever spikes.

Bryson, once vibrant and full of life, started exhibiting signs of distress- his appetite waned, his energy dwindled, and the spark in his eyes flickered under the weight of illness. There was a noticeable absence of joy. Frustration rose within me as another week went by, and despite all my efforts, I couldn't alleviate his suffering. Amidst the relentless sicknesses, I clung to a semblance of normalcy by ensuring Bryson's therapist continued their visits. It was my desire to see him achieve his developmental milestones.

Monday morning dawned after a challenging weekend, during which I had minimal sleep, consumed by worry and constant care of Bryson. Occupational therapy, a weekly fixture on Mondays, was scheduled to arrive at nine in the morning. Considering the strain of the past days, I decided to let Bryson sleep a bit longer until her arrival. However, when I went back to wake him up, a sinking feeling enveloped me. I couldn't rouse him. Given his occasional lethargy attributed to his seizure medication and the rough weekend we had experienced, I initially attributed it to that. As moments passed without a response, I knew something was seriously wrong. In a panic, I called Brad and my mother. While on the phone, Linda picked Bryson up and held him. Brad, working only three minutes from our house, hurried home and together we rushed him to the hospital about ten minutes from our home.

The doctors at the hospital were unable to pinpoint the cause of Bryson's distress. Swiftly, he was transferred to another hospital, a one-hour drive away, prompting another ambulance ride that plunged us once again into the disconcerting realm of uncertainty about our son's well-being. Fear gripped me; the thought of losing my son was unbearable, and memories of his first ambulance ride flooded my mind- the fear, the unknown, the hard.

Arriving at a new hospital, we were directed to take a specific elevator, yet nobody seemed to know exactly where Bryson was located. Anxiety surged as I frantically searched the long white hallways, driven by an urgent need to find him and ensure his safety. As his mother, the responsibility was heavily on me - I had to make sure he was okay.

Finally reaching the Pediatric ICU, my heart sank at the sight of my little boy. Tubes from the ventilator and other monitors snaked around him. Wearing a light blue gown with the words "laundry services" embroidered on its chest, he appeared almost lifeless, and my heart groaned from the weight of the situation. Questions tormented me - What could I have done differently to prevent us from being here? I grappled again with self-blame, constantly turning the burden on myself, feeling that I hadn't done enough. Despite my vow to be strong and do everything for my son, I found myself in a state of helplessness, unable to do anything except pray, but prayer eluded me in the moment. All I could do was question God in the face of these overwhelming challenges before us.

Eventually, he was diagnosed with respiratory syncytial virus (RSV). He endured four days on the ventilator, and on the second day, a risky attempt to wean him off failed, as his lungs weren't ready. We came perilously close to losing him that day. Fueled by the fighting spirit that had been his lifelong companion, Bryson rallied back from the brink. On the fifth day, he was transferred to the pediatric ward, marking a significant step in his recovery. My mother paid a visit to her little man. She brought along a small stuffed Boston Terrier puppy named Moxie, resembling our real dog Cronin. Moxie found a place under Bryson's left arm, close to his face, offering a comforting presence.

Amid these dark moments, God used this situation for good. While in the ICU, we discovered a newborn baby with similar stroke symptoms. Connecting with the parents revealed that, like Bryson, their daughter had been diagnosed with having a stroke in utero. We shared our journey, providing them comfort and courage as they embarked on a path we had navigated 18 months prior. We exchanged contact information and maintained a connection for many years.

God in His wisdom and plan placed us in that hospital for "a time as this"

In the month preceding Bryson's bout with RSV, I continued to document in my ordinary binder all the relentless array of appointments - therapy, bloodwork, evaluations, doctor visits, and an EEG. I also chronicled all the excessive seizure activity, along with documenting symptoms of colds, coughs, and prescribed medication. Yet, hidden within the tumultuous sea of negative entries, there was one day that stood out. I had scrawled, "Bryson started scooting on his butt!' It was a moment of celebration, a triumph hidden among the hardships that dominated the other days. This precious note served as a poignant reminder that even during the overwhelm, there were pockets of joy and accomplishment, though brief, which provided the spark of hope and resilience.

As we drove toward the neurologist's office, I turned on my blinker and exited onto Nimtz Parkway. This drive always felt like a heavy weight. The quarterly appointments, combined with the regular sleep deprived EEG tests, means I could drive this route in my sleep. The toll of RSV, combined with the heavy seizure medication and ongoing seizures, continued to assail Bryson's immune system. His eyes remained dim and void of life, and any fleeting moment when the spark of life would briefly reappear, we were reminded of the precious spirit within him. Brad and I wanted to explore every possible avenue that could benefit him.

Opening the back hatch of our minivan, I pulled out Bryson's colorful stroller, his trusty companion. Brad placed Bryson into the stroller, and we walked up toward the one-story neurologist's office.

It wasn't long before Bryson's name was called, and we went through the paces of weight, height, temperature. After the neurologist arrived, we dove deep into a discussion about what the next step could be to get control of Bryson's seizures. "We could start the Ketogenic diet" the neurologist suggested. He went on to explain what that involved. "The ketogenic diet is a high-fat, low-carb diet that has been used as a therapeutic intervention for controlling seizures. The primary goal is to induce a state of ketosis, where the body shifts from using glucose as its primary energy source to relying on ketones, which are produced from the breakdown of fats." As I absorbed the information, my first thoughts were *this couldn't be too bad.* The neurologist continued explaining that we would have to hospitalize Bryson to get him into ketosis. Brad and I looked at each other and sighed. We decided before we even left the appointment that we would give this diet a try.

As we wrestled with decisions regarding Bryson's health, Brad and I found ourselves contemplating the prospect of bringing another Plett into the world. Fear reared its ugly head as concerns about a recurrence of Bryson's situation surfaced. Medical assurances eased concerns about genetic factors. Trusting in Almighty God, I became pregnant again.

Five months after Bryson's scare with RSV, we were in another hospital room, but this time, Bryson entered healthy. I was in the beginning stages of pregnancy and feeling more worn down. Thankfully, his favorite Aunt Shirley from Manitoba came down to help entertain him for the few days it would take to achieve ketosis. Bryson's first meal that evening arrived from the cafeteria. The plate had a note that said "NOTHING." Bryson had to fast for several meals to start the process. This was torture for me, withholding food, and he was so young he didn't understand the why behind it. I stayed in his room overnight, another restless night of struggling to know if we were doing the right thing.

As the next day dawned and foods could be introduced, I learned that his diet would consist primarily of foods like butter, applesauce, hot dogs, and heavy whipping cream. I was given pages of menu ideas for Bryson and connected with several professionals who could help me navigate this new way of eating. Bryson didn't grumble or complain, he just ate the food placed in front of him. Two days later, we exited the hospital on a totally unique adventure.

Bryson maintained his medication routine and continued with his array of therapies, including the addition of music therapy to go along with his occupational, physical, developmental, and speech therapies. Ear infections persisted, leading to the insertion of tubes in his ears. Despite the looming exhaustion and the persistent symptoms of pregnancy, I donned a smiling mask and pushed forward.

> **Courage doesn't always roar. Sometimes courage is the quiet voice at the end of the day saying, "I will try again tomorrow." Mary Ann Radmacher**[7]

As the calendar turned, almost a year into the grueling journey of the ketogenic diet, Bryson's resilience was undeniable, but the toll on his body was apparent. Navigating the complexities of this diet had been a hellish experience, filled with moments of doubt and the persistent desire to give up. Yet, a steadfast belief lingered – a hope that all the efforts invested would eventually yield positive results with his seizures. Bryson's hair had changed to an almost white hue, a visual representation of the physiological changes his body underwent in this altered metabolic state.

Therapists continued entering our home weekly to assist Bryson in reaching his developmental goals. However, Bryson's health took a downward turn. He started experiencing diarrhea and vomiting. The toll on his small body was evident, and the frustration and exhaustion weighed heavily on me.

During these trials, in that seemingly ordinary binder, I wrote on May 10, 2000 "little brother born!" Through the haze of challenges, the arrival of Tyrell, our second son, brought a glimmer of happiness though it couldn't dispel the unrelenting tempo of daily life.

I was grateful that Tyrell's birth, marked by a scheduled c-section, unfolded smoothly. Several days later, I returned home. But even in returning home with a newborn, my focus was immediately back to documenting Bryson's fevers, sore throat, coughing, and bloodwork appointment. Brad and my mother stepped in to share the caregiving responsibilities, providing relief amid the chaos.

Two weeks after Tyrell's birth, Bryson's fragile health led to hospitalization for dehydration. The cruel reality set in – the Ketogenic Diet, initially pursued with hope, had proved to be more detrimental than beneficial for Bryson. With a heavy heart, we made the difficult decision to slowly transition him out of ketosis and back to a more conventional eating plan.

Survival mode became a way of life, and several months after Tyrell's birth, an overwhelming fatigue and persistent sadness gripped me, making each day a struggle. Despite the inner voice urging me to be strong, I recognized that living in this state of mind was unsustainable. Acknowledging the need for help, I eventually sought out counseling.

In the first session, the counselor started with questions about my life. In a matter of minutes, I unburdened myself of the multitude of struggles I had been carrying – the challenges of motherhood, raising Bryson, helping manage a business, and supporting my mom through her continued grief over the loss of my father and her caregiving role of Joanna. The weight of it all had become unbearable, and I felt overwhelmed.

It didn't take long for the counselor to gently point out, "Lisa, you are showing all the signs of depression." Although I had heard of postpartum depression, vocalizing my struggles in that moment served as a wake-up call. I was carrying a heavy load, and the realization that I was indeed experiencing depression prompted a resolute decision within me – I didn't want to succumb to this, and I was determined to overcome it.

I made the deliberate effort to confront and conquer depression head-on. Through several counseling sessions, I learned about the importance of asking for help. This was a difficult step to take, especially since my mother was already providing considerable assistance. However, I allowed her to shoulder more of the burden of the household chores, such as laundry and cooking, to alleviate some of my burden.

In addition to seeking external support, my counselor explained the importance of self-care. I learned to grant myself permission to rest by taking naps while the boys were asleep, even if only for a few minutes. I also communicated with Brad, asking for dedicated time several nights a week to indulge in a hot bath, allowing myself to relax and breathe.

Armed with the tools and insights gained from counseling, I dedicated myself to incorporating them into my daily routine, striving to prioritize my mental well-being. Gradually, I started to observe glimmers of hope and joy, even as the grip of grief and overwhelm persisted. Although I had gained practical strategies to lift myself from the depth of depression, my efforts were only surface-deep. I had yet to invest the time and effort needed to delve into the wounds concealed beneath the surface. During this challenging period, I firmly believe that God carried me. He knew that the timing wasn't right for me to confront the deep-seated hurts of my past, which had shaped the way I navigated life. With His gentle grace, He provided the strength to endure and overcome, empowering me to care for my boys with love and resilience.

In a Stroke of Love

> **Courage is not having the strength to go on; it is going on when you don't have the strength. Theodore Roosevelt[8]**

We had taken Bryson off the ketogenic diet, what next? Brad and I found ourselves again taking the exit onto Nimtz Parkway to the neurologist. Our neurologist had a firm belief that he could *cure* Bryson's epilepsy. In my exhausted and naïve brain, we trusted and believed a cure was possible. Bryson's health had improved in the months since he had gotten off the ketogenic diet, our hearts were relieved to see more spark and spunk in him.

"My recommendation is brain surgery to remove the part causing the seizures," the neurologist suggested as we sat in his office. Brad and I looked at each other in shock and disbelief. Those words sent shivers down my spine. Surgery? We wanted a cure, but at what cost? Still in shock, we left the office and drove home. It didn't take us long to know in our hearts and minds, this wasn't the answer. We needed a second opinion.

Our quest for a second opinion led us to the revered halls of Cleveland Clinic. Amidst the confusion of deciding where to turn, extensive research pointed us to a well renowned neurologist. Gratitude along with anticipation and impatience lingered as we awaited his neurology appointment, scheduled months in advance.

The journey to Cleveland Clinic was a two-day affair. Brad and I, a determined duo, lifted prayers, yearning for this to be the answer we sought. The first day involved an EEG and blood work, each moment stretching the taut thread of hope. The next day held the promise of answers as we set to meet with the neurologist.

The hospital building, though aged, held a distinctive charm. The exam room walls were a faded yellow color. Basic white and beige striped curtains hung over the one window in the back of the room, the curtains added a touch of simplicity to the complex emotions that surrounded us. As the neurologist entered, a breath of fresh air swept into the room, a stark contrast to our initial encounter with the first neurologist. Her demeanor exuded kindness and care, a comforting presence amidst our storm. She delivered a harsh reality- there was no cure for epilepsy as we had been told could be accomplished. However, her optimism sparked, and after examining Bryson's test results, she proposed a plan – with continued medication, we could gain control over this seizure activity. There was even the hopeful prospect that, with time, we might be able to gradually wean him off all seizure medication, allowing us to observe how he fared without the heavy medicine burden. The prospect of a future where Bryson could potentially navigate life with reduced reliance on medication breathed a newfound sense of optimism in our hearts.

A surge of anger and frustration coursed through me as the realization hit. What if Bryson could be walking and talking already without this heavy medication burden? The years of striving, pushing for improvement, and countless attempts to cure his epilepsy flashed before my eyes. What had we done? The new neurologist, in her compassion, couldn't comprehend the extensive medication regimen Bryson was on. She reduced several of his medications at the first visit, unveiling a potential improvement in his quality of life and abilities. Remarkably, Bryson's health took a positive turn, and progress became evident in all aspects of his life.

Once again, Brad and I found ourselves contemplating the idea of expanding our family to include a third child. In the early years of our marriage, we had envisioned four children as the ideal number. It wasn't long before the pregnancy test confirmed our hopes, and I embarked on my third pregnancy journey.

Kaden made his entrance into the world three weeks early on April 5, 2003, prompting momentary concerns of lung function and the need for oxygen support. The emotional rollercoaster of potential health issues resurfaced, flooding my mind with memories of Bryson's challenges. "Not again, God," I silently pleaded. Miraculously, Kaden's lungs showed improvement on the second day, bringing a wave of relief and gratitude. Now a mother of three boys- Bryson, at the age of five, Tyrell at three, both attending preschool and newborn Kaden- my already busy life catapulted to the next level.

As Bryson continued to make strides in his therapies and overall health, I recalled the doctor's words about the possibility of eventually discontinuing all seizure medication. With each improvement, I felt increasingly convinced that the time was ripe to explore this possibility. I contacted the neurologist, and she wholeheartedly agreed. We initiated a withdrawal plan! A few months into the plan, I sensed God telling me to stop all his medications, and without doctor authorization, that was what I did in August 2003. Over the next few years, we continued regular check-ups with the neurologist from Cleveland Clinic, witnessing Bryson's remarkable health. In 2005, we were completely discharged from neurology care. We gave testimony to God's healing touch on Bryson, freeing him from epilepsy.

For years following our initial appointment with Bryson's new neurologist, every drive past Nimtz Parkway off the bypass reignited a storm of anger, regret, and the ugly feeling of self-blame. The mere sight of it became a trigger, evoking memories of the critical decisions made at the doctor's office during those first years. Many questions surfaced. Did the doctor truly have Bryson's best interest at heart? Or, was his pursuit fueled by the desire for personal acclaim? Should we have known better? Should I have been more vigilant in questioning the doctors' intentions? Why did I trust his medical expertise? As a parent, I bore the weight of responsibility to do what was best for my child. I wanted to believe that I did the best I could with the knowledge I had at the time, but the nagging question always lingered. What if, unknowingly, I had cost Bryson something vital?

Navigating the various challenges in Bryson's journey felt like traveling a road with unexpected twists, turns, and potholes. I thought I had left the road of seizures for good, but after five years of being free from seizure medication and seizures, Bryson experienced unusual episodes at school and during a Christmas vacation trip to Canada. Deep down, I knew what they were - *seizures*. However, I didn't want to acknowledge it. I had publicly declared his healing back in 2005, "We stand firmly believing that God healed Bryson from Epilepsy." Facing this road again seemed inconceivable. I struggled with questions, not wanting to doubt the healing hand of God, but we were back again on the road I didn't want to travel. I wanted to believe in His plan for Bryson.

During this time, I was reading through the Bible chronologically. I found inspiration in Abraham's questioning and pleading with the Lord in Genesis 18:1- 21:7. The question in Genesis 18:14 echoed in my mind: "Is anything too hard for the Lord?" I felt God speaking through these scriptures, assuring me that nothing is too hard for Him, and He would be with me as I traversed the roads ahead. He welcomed my questions and doubts, offering me His unwavering love.

Reluctantly, I called the neurologist to discuss the next steps, leading us back on the road of seizure medications. The twice-a-day seizure medicine routine became a necessary part of his health maintenance.

The road had been filled with curves, each bump causing its share of pain. On the day we restarted seizure medication, I committed to walking step by step with God, trusting that nothing is too hard for Him. I knew He could make the roads smooth and straight; all I needed to do was walk with my hand firmly held in His! It wasn't easy, and there were moments when I took my hands out of His and tried to solve it on my own. His outstretched hand always remained, patiently waiting for me to grab hold again.

In the NICU at Riley hospital, amidst the weight of Bryson's diagnosis, information inundated us about programs that could support us on this unexpected journey. Among them, the First Steps program run by the state, offered therapeutic services to aid Bryson's development. The initiation of this program marked the beginning of a deluge of appointments that would shape the next five years of our lives.

Bryson had started physical therapy at a mere six weeks old, followed by occupational therapy at six months, and developmental and speech therapy at eleven months. The remarkable ladies who became a consistent presence in our home, working tirelessly with Bryson, became not just therapists but integral parts of our lives. Play, which should be a carefree aspect of childhood, became intentional and goal-oriented. Bryson, just a baby and then a toddler, engaged in play that was designed to push his boundaries and explore his capabilities. As a mother, I found myself on the sidelines, observing with gratitude the dedication of these women who had chosen a profession that sought to help children like Bryson. Yet, simultaneously, there was an undercurrent of discouragement, a constant wondering about the extent of Bryson's accomplishments, given the slow and uncertain process. Every appointment, I had to put on a façade of normalcy, greeting someone from the outside while inwardly wrestling with the reality that my son faced many limitations.

A fierce battle raged within me, a clash between denial and acceptance. Every fiber of my being yearned to believe that he would overcome all the side effects of his stroke. I desperately wanted to hold onto the reassuring illusion that everything would eventually work out for Bryson's good. The weight of uncertainty pressed heavily on my heart, and during this internal struggle, hope and fear danced on the fragile string of my emotions.

While the First Steps program within the school system offered excellent therapists, their resources were limited. It became evident that Bryson needed more intensive therapy. Through references, we reached out to a private physical pediatric therapist. No longer did we have the convenience of a therapist coming into our home. We now had to travel thirty minutes each way for Bryson to receive these services. It was during this time that my mother stepped in again, graciously handling the back-and-forth drive for Bryson's therapy, easing the burden on me as I managed the responsibilities at home.

Balancing the desire for Bryson's best care and the need to experience the joys of family life became a delicate juggling act.

At the age of four, Bryson, with the unwavering assistance of his physical therapist, achieved the milestone of walking with braces – an occasion of celebration for our family. The journey was not without challenges, a broken right shoulder during a session working on steps, but we persevered.

Speech was a formidable struggle for Bryson, and his patient speech therapist, Lori, employed various strategies, including picture boards and basic sign language. As Bryson entered school age, the First Steps program concluded, and we decided to hire Lori privately to continue his therapy. The hard work paid off when, at the age of eight, Bryson found his voice, forming words and sentences. Although his speech was challenging to understand at times, the ability to communicate became a source of immeasurable joy in our lives.

A sentiment from a fellow special needs mom resonated deeply, "I just wanted a day when no one came to the house; a day without PT, OT, ST, and nurses. I just wanted a day when we could just be family." I echoed her sentiment, acknowledging that if we were to follow every recommendation from the doctors and therapists, our children wouldn't have a life.

As the years unfolded, Bryson's determined spirit shone through. The years of therapy equipped him with the skills to walk, run, and speak. Every step he took and every word he said served as a testament to his determination and strength.

As I sifted through the pages of that unassuming white binder containing the chronicles of Bryson's first three years, preparing to write this chapter, I couldn't help but feel the weight of those tumultuous years pressing down on me. It was almost incomprehensible to fathom how I had managed to traverse through it all. Beside the binder lay a "baby's first year calendar" that I had eagerly purchased before his birth. Most of its pages remained blank, the bright stickers left untouched. Yet, here and there, I noticed a few stickers haphazardly placed on some of the pages to signify an accomplishment. In that moment, I was transported back to my younger self, filled with the hopeful anticipation of motherhood, yearning to fill the pages with joyous memories. However, grief washed over me as I reflected on the unfulfilled desires of that 26-year-old version of myself.

Clutching both the binder and the calendar in my hands, I sat in the corner of Bryson's room in a state of deep reflection. Despite the medical and physical challenges that Bryson had faced, he had endured and triumphed. Despite the grief, fear, and overwhelm that I had faced, I also had endured and triumphed. While I longed for the brightness of those stickers and the simplicity of the easier path, I recognized the profound truth embedded within the scribbled entries of that white binder. Those entries helped shape me into the woman I am today. The binder, a testament of God's unwavering faithfulness, His constant presence, a beacon of protection and provision throughout the difficult years.

CHAPTER 5
Family Ties

Family isn't an important thing. It's everything."
Michael J. Fox[9]

"Mom, I want to run this race with Bryson. The top 10 get medals, and everyone gets a ribbon," stated Ty as he handed me a paper from school announcing a cross-country run for elementary kids at the high school. It was a chance for the elementary kids to experience a one-mile run with high school coaches overseeing. While I appreciated Ty's desire to run with his brother, a thought crossed my mind – does Ty understand Bryson's limitations? "Ty, have you thought about asking your friend Trent or Cousin Tucker to run with you?" I replied. Ty responded quickly "Why not just with Bryson?" I pointed out Bryson might struggle to finish. "Mom, it's okay, I don't need a medal; we'll still get a ribbon."

Sacrifice and love emanated from my sweet Ty. He was willing to give up a shot at a medal to run with his brother. His heart longed to see Bryson participate and succeed. It struck me that Ty understood it wasn't about winning; it was about participating and completing the race.

As I reflected on this exchange later that evening, I realized how several of my insecurities from childhood had surfaced, revealing my perspective on Bryson. While I was focused on Bryson's physical limitations, Ty had perceived an opportunity for him to participate. My lens captured the world's emphasis on winning races, whereas Ty recognized the significance of Bryson believing in himself, uttering the affirmations, "I can do this" and "I'm important enough," despite the handicaps and hurdles.

Memories also flooded my mind of me wanting to play on the basketball team in junior high. I could feel my body tense as I recalled the fear I felt of potential ridicule and being different as a child. I didn't want him running in the race because I couldn't bear the thought of Bryson experiencing any of those emotions; I needed to shield him from such pain. In that poignant moment, a wave of shame enveloped me. Fear had kept me on the sidelines, not participating in activities as a child, and fear was still present. Here I stood, a 39-year-old mother projecting these same insecurities onto my own child-a stark realization.

Engulfed in my shame, I was able to acknowledge how God uses our children to teach us essential lessons. Ty's perspective served as a reminder that I needed to shift my mindset. While my rational mind grasped Bryson's inherent value and love, the emotional remnants of my own insecurities were clouding how I parented Bryson. I also realized how I lacked the ability to see myself as valuable and loved. Understanding that if I wanted to impart the lesson of self-worth to my children, I had to lead by example. It was clear to me that my trek toward self-acceptance would be fundamental in teaching them to do the same. Tears falling, I cried out to God. I acknowledged my shame and my struggle to see myself as valuable and worthy of love, asking for His guidance in helping me be the best mother I could for my boys.

I recognized that my difficulties navigating the world of disabilities stemmed from my challenging childhood experiences with my aunt Joanna. I yearned for my boys to be a part of Bryson's world, yet I struggled with the memories of not wanting to be a part of Joanna's world. Her world was awkward and different. This internal conflict revealed itself in my hesitation to push Ty and Kaden to attend Bryson's special Olympic events, events that I struggled to attend. As a mother, I still didn't want to be in that world, and I didn't want my boys to have those same thoughts. Gratefully, my boys didn't notice my insecurities. They occasionally attended Bryson's events, demonstrating their unconditional love for him. However, I denied them the opportunity to truly be a part of his world

As a mother with many fears, I was adamant about protecting my boys from needless injuries. I had endured enough challenges. Knowing the typical inclination for boys to roughhouse, I often intervened, not allowing Ty and Kaden to engage in such play with Bryson, and even limited their interactions with each other. Yet, in doing so, I inadvertently hindered them from the ability to connect with Bryson on a more genuine and unfiltered level.

Brad and I had frequent discussions about Ty, contemplating the impact of Bryson's medical needs, and Kaden, a younger child in constant need for my time and energy. The question loomed large – would Tyrell feel neglected in our family? We also wrestled with the idea that Ty, being the middle child, was inadvertently shouldering the responsibilities of a firstborn due to Bryson's unique needs. As parents, we wondered if these roles would present challenges for Ty as he matured, compounded by the additional role of being a sibling to a special needs brother.

Yet, amid our concerns, we recognized that God gifted us with a remarkable son in Ty. Calm, sensitive, and caring, he didn't carve the spotlight, never demanding. As Bryson's middle brother, Ty embraced his role with genuine care and love, extending these same qualities to all who considered him family or friend.

Kaden, the youngest, brought a different energy to our household: silly, outgoing, and mischievous! Despite their different personalities, a strong bond formed between Ty and Kaden, rooted in their shared love for the outdoors and adventure- a passion inherited from Brad.

However, as the boys aged, my lack of adventurous spirit led to me feeling left behind as Brad and the boys embarked on exciting adventures. I couldn't ignore the widening gap. I harbored jealousy while I was left behind with Bryson, and his unique needs constrained his ability to participate in these adventures. I found myself stuck in the disability world, a world I had experienced as a teenager and desperately didn't want then and didn't want now for both me and my son. The stark contrast between what I perceived as "normal," and the reality of my circumstances left me yearning for a normal family life that seemed elusive in our unique family dynamic.

> **We can rejoice, too, when we run into problems and trials, for we know that they help us develop endurance. And endurance develops strength of character, and character strengthens our confident hope of salvation. Romans 5:3-4**

Monday morning dawned, the golden rays of August sunlight streaming through the large windows, casting a warm glow on the worn tan carpet of the living room. The air hung heavy with the scent of detergent. The previous week had marked the return to school for both Bryson and Ty, with Bryson attending kindergarten in a functional skills classroom and Ty attending the local Montessori preschool. Finally, I found myself anticipating moments of uninterrupted time with three-month-old Kaden as the summer had whirled by in a flurry of activities and the demands of caring for a newborn. Finishing folding the towels, I took a well-deserved break, sinking into the comfort of the blue rocker chair nestled in the corner, cradling Kaden in my arms.

Just as the stillness settled, the shrill ring of the phone pierced the air. Hurrying to silence the ring so as not to awaken Kaden, I picked up the phone off the arm of the chair. "Hello," I answered. "Hi Lisa, this is Dan. Brad had been involved in an accident at a job site." Dan calmly spoke into the phone. Dan was the president of our family business. His words caused an immediate jolt of panic. Fear gripped my heart, threatening to choke out my breath. "What happened? Is he okay?" I questioned. "Brad was in a ditch at a job site, and the dirt caved in on him. He was buried up to his thighs. The other worker with him gave Brad a phone, and I've been talking to him. The ambulance is on the way to the job site." Words escaped me in that moment, and I hung up the phone.

With Kaden still in my arms, I called my mother and briefly told her what happened. I asked her to come immediately to take care of Kaden. Shock settled in, numbing my senses, but I knew I had to change my clothes and head to the hospital as soon as my mom arrived. *Wait, what hospital is he being taken to?* I suddenly thought. Hastily, I called Dan back and he clarified, the ambulance was coming to Goshen Hospital.

As I drove to the hospital, a surge of disbelief entered my mind. *This can't be happening.* I found myself suspended in a disorienting reality, a feeling of floating away from the familiar ground of life. Memories of Bryson's hospital visits flashed through my mind. The short drive to the hospital felt like forever, and fear about Brad's well-being created a knot in the pit of my stomach. Despite the fog, with trembling hands, I managed to dial our pastor's number, the brief call serving as a lifeline. Conveying the few details of the accident was a plea for support.

Entering through the emergency room doors, I was greeted by the sounds of a TV playing in the waiting room and the antiseptic smell. I hurriedly approached the front desk. "Is Brad Plett here? The kind receptionist typed into her computer and said, "He is en route, and the ambulance should be here shortly. Have a seat. I will let you know when he arrives. *Sit down? How can I sit down while my husband is hurt?* Thoughts swirled in my head. I forced myself into a chair, and minutes dragged on slowly as I waited anxiously for the ambulance to arrive. Pastor Mel, a reassuring presence, joined me, providing me a sense of peace.

Finally, a nurse approached me, "Your husband has arrived; you can come back to his room." A mixture of relief and anticipation flooded through my body. I followed her into the room that housed my husband. There, in the center of the stark white room, lay my husband draped in a crisp white sheet, the air carrying an underlying tension. He tried to smile, but the visible pain he was experiencing was written all over his face. Rushing to his side, my eyes betraying the traces of worry and fear, I laid my head on his chest, seeking the familiar comfort of his frame. Brad slowly placed his arm on my back, and finding solace in the embrace, we stayed there for a few minutes. Unspoken words hovered in the air, carrying the weight of the situation.

Immediately after entering the ER, Brad had undergone all the vital tests to determine the extent of his injuries. Shortly after my arrival, the ER doctor entered the room, " Brad, your pelvis is broken, several of the lower vertebrae are cracked, and there are cracks in your left hip." The news was shattering but carried a sign of relief. No internal injuries.

Brad and I were left alone in the room as the hospital started the process of getting him admitted. The phone hung on the back wall, and one by one, I called my family and Brad's family members and close friends. A nurse entered the room, "We need a urine sample to finalize the admitting process," she said. As I assisted Brad with the sample, pain written on his face, what emptied into the cup was blood mixed with urine. Alarm and fear surfaced, jolting the room like an electric current. I anxiously called in the nurse. Brad's eyes now betrayed a flicker of fear; my trembling hands reached out to grab a hold of his hand. The uncertainty of the future loomed large.

In a whirlwind of panic, tests confirmed a torn urethra, prompting immediate surgery. A super pubic catheter was inserted, a lifeline for Brad's basic bodily functions. During the hours he spent in surgery, I found peace in the company of friends and family who came to sit with me. Grateful that I wasn't navigating this moment alone, their presence provided comfort. Exhaustion weighed heavily on me, both physically and emotionally, yet I felt the unwavering support and prayers of my village.

Before Brad's release from the hospital, Brad's urologist disclosed that had they not discovered the torn urethra when they did, the consequences could have been fatal. Stunned by the stark reality of how close Brad had come to dying, a wave of gratitude swept over us, and we thanked God for His miraculous intervention.

Five days after the accident and surgery, I brought Brad home to a hospital bed in our living room. The weight of responsibility intensified. Along with my three boys, one a newborn, now I had a husband unable to move without assistance and requiring care. Days turned into weeks, and with every passing moment, with feelings of overwhelm and exhaustion present, God provided support through family and friends and many prayers for healing. In what seemed an endless six weeks of pain and perseverance, Brad's pelvis mended. Although pain lingered, normal life beckoned again.

Brad slowly resumed light duties at work but continued the use of the super pubic catheter. We knew that, eventually, he would have to undergo urethra reconstructive surgery. On an early December day, four months after the accident, Brad underwent surgery at the University of Chicago. The surgery was a success, and Brad was finally able to remove the catheter in January of 2004.

The weight of responsibilities in the aftermath of Brad's accident could have easily sent me spiraling downward into depression, reminiscent of the challenging times I faced after Ty was born. Instead, I embraced the defensive stance I learned early in life. Strength became my refuge, concealing emotions for survival. A resilient determination surfaced within me. I adopted a new belief, one that I tied my worth to: the conviction that I had to single-handedly manage and attend to all the responsibilities placed on me. Despite the support of my village, I felt an overwhelming sense of responsibility, believing that "I have to do it all" rested squarely on my shoulders.

As I embraced the arrival of 2004, I did so with a heart infused with renewed hope, yearning for a sense of normalcy after the tumultuous events of the past year. However, the winter months, with their snowy landscapes and biting cold, brought with them the familiar companions of sickness, colds, and coughs. After several bouts of sickness, a persistent cough became an unwelcome companion to Brad. Multiple pneumonia diagnoses and rounds of medication failed to alleviate the bothersome symptoms. Brad's doctor recommended further testing. An unsettling feeling settled within me, and my mind became a whirlwind of possible scenarios, each one contributing to the growing angst in my stomach.

The drive to Brad's appointment with a pulmonologist was filled with tension and silence. As we were escorted into the examination room, sitting side by side, the air seemed to thicken with each passing moment, a palpable tension that mirrored the weight of the impending medical diagnosis. Intertwining my fingers with Brads, silently stating the commitment to face whatever news lay ahead as a united front.

Several weeks earlier, as we lay in bed enveloped by the darkness, Brad's admission of fears lingered in the air, "I'm afraid it will be CANCER," he confessed, his words, a heavy whisper, bounced through the stillness of the room. Now, in the stark reality of the doctor's office, the memory of that intimate conversation flashed in our minds. The doctor was known for his expertise in oncology. With the connection between Brad's earlier fears and the specialized field of the doctor we were about to consult, there was only one viable explanation that made sense in our minds.

"Brad, you have a rare birth defect called Pulmonary Sequestration, a medical condition characterized by a mass of non-functioning lung tissue that does not communicate with the normal airways. It can present itself with respiratory symptoms, recurrent infections, or complications like pneumonia." The doctor's words hung in the air as the diagnosis settled into our minds, and I felt a release of the breath I had been holding. I wanted to shout with joy that Brad didn't have cancer, yet the weight of the rare condition cast a shadow over the room, reminding me that the journey ahead held its own set of new challenges.

The doctor emphasized the rarity of this lung defect, expressing a level of discomfort in performing the necessary surgery. The decision was made to schedule the surgery at Indiana University Hospital in Indianapolis, a hospital where a surgeon renowned for their expertise in navigating the intricate complexities of Brad's condition worked.

The weight of another impending surgery bore down on me, igniting a surge of anger. *Not again*, I thought, *not another stretch of time where the weight of responsibility for everything rested solely on my shoulders*. When, I wondered, would I catch a break? Exhaustion and overwhelm draped over me like a heavy cloud. I grappled with the nature of God's plan, wrestling with the heaviness of it all. Fear, my unwelcome companion, gripped me tightly. The reality of having been close to losing him just the year before haunted my thoughts, and the impending complexity of this surgery intensified my anxiety.

As we approached the end of another year, surgery was on the docket again. On the road to Indianapolis, a tense silence enveloped the car. I was trapped in the fear of losing my husband. Finally, unable to contain my fear any longer, I asked, "Brad, how are you feeling about the surgery? I am scared." Brad remained silent for a few moments and then replied, "I'm in a win-win situation, Lisa. If I die, I'm with my Heavenly Father, and if I live, I get to live with you." I was taken aback as I grasped his response. "But what about me? If you die, I'm left with the kids" I uttered in sheer fear. His response did little to alleviate the overwhelming fear that enveloped me like a suffocating coat. The past few years had been a relentless journey full of trauma, and I found myself hanging on-physically, emotionally, and mentally- by a thread. The fear of losing my husband loomed large, casting a shadow over the moment. Brad, sensing my distress, did his best to provide comfort, yet the anxiety and fear remained relentless. The frailty of my emotions was obvious, a silent plea echoing within me, "*I can't lose my husband.*"

Support from family provided a comforting presence during the agonizing wait during surgery. The surgery was long and complex but successful, as the surgeon removed the bottom part of his left lung. Memories flashed through my mind as I entered Brad's room shortly after he returned from recovery. Again, his body, still and vulnerable, lay against the crisp white sheets, his physical form revealing the aftermath of the surgery. Wires and tubes tethered him to the bed. Combined with the look of pain in his eyes, there was an undeniable sense of relief I saw in his face. Taking his hand, I felt his warmth. Leaning over, I pressed a gentle kiss on his forehead, a silent expression of the emotions that words could scarcely capture.

Thankfully, family stayed by my side as we sat together beside Brad's bed. The doctor kept saying that he was recovering well, but the tests were showing that he was not ready to come home. On evenings in my hotel room, exhaustion warred against my anxiety, and sleep would not come. The desire that I needed to be strong clashed with an inner longing for safety and comfort. The battle within me raged, "*Would anyone ever take care of me?*" Yet again, faced with the weight of responsibilities, I found the strength to endure. My husband and family needed me.

As Christmas approached, anxiety mounted, fueled by the fear of not making it home in time to celebrate Christmas with the boys. However, the morning before Christmas, Brad received clearance to leave the hospital. The joy that accompanied our reunion as a family that night was immeasurable. Grateful tears welled in my eyes, knowing that despite the challenges ahead, the gift of having my husband with us was the true essence of the season.

As I lifted my praises to God, thanking him for the gift of His son Jesus -the real reason for Christmas- I felt a profound sense of having received a precious and invaluable present that year: the restored health of my husband.

CHAPTER 6
Special Education

> *"If we cannot teach the sciences; we can, at any rate, employ the dim twilight of the slow developing mind in pressing home the value of truth , honesty, and purity; let us tell of the love of God, the salvation of Christ, and the guidance and comfort of the Holy Spirit. Let us do this conscientiously and await the dawn of the mind sun; when the sun rises, it may be more beautiful, more lovely than we ever could have imagined. Our toil will be a thousand times repaid, not perhaps by the successful result of a competitive examination, but by the useful, loving, and healthy life."*
> E. Downes, MD in the Parents Review, November 1897[10]

The REACH preschool room was bursting with colors, a vibrant space designed to stimulate the young minds. Educational posters with basic shapes, colors, numbers, and alphabet letters, adorn the walls. I slowly pushed two-and-half-year-old Bryson in his compact stroller, decorated in bright and lively colors, into the classroom. This was his first IEP meeting. REACH preschool was operated by the county's Special Education Department, called ECSEC. Low, child-sized tables and chairs populated the center of the room, and I made my way over to the table, already occupied by several special education personnel and the preschool teacher. Pulling away a chair to accommodate Bryson's stroller, I attempted to position my larger frame into the small chair. Lighthearted chatter commenced as we prepared to get to the official business at hand. My hands were sweaty, and I didn't know what to expect. I had experiences in the medical and therapy world, but the educational process was a new road to travel.

This first IEP meeting was to gather information about Bryson so that the special education department could determine the services he needed. We hadn't gotten past the introductions when Bryson became antsy. Quietly, the classroom teacher pulled Bryson away from the table and helped him out of his stroller by one of the learning centers. As soon as she had Bryson happily playing with building blocks, she returned to the table and the conversation. Bryson's presence there was important for the educators to observe him and understand beyond my words how Bryson was doing.

"Lisa, can you give a brief description of Bryson?" Susan, the preschool teacher, asked. I had repeated these words before, and the words rolled off my tongue with ease. "Bryson suffered a medical event, a stroke in utero, which resulted in seizures. The stroke also has affected the right side of his body, which has delayed his walking and crawling. His main mode of transportation is scooting on his butt. His right arm and hand have minimal strength and function, and he is nonverbal."

Many more questions followed, and it seemed as if I had divulged every conceivable detail about Bryson. As we approached the end of the application process, a significant question presented itself. "What do we write down as his diagnosis?" Susan inquired and continued, "We don't want to label him too much now. We don't want to put limitations on him because this could affect services down the road."

I struggled to understand this concept, seeking clarification from all the people involved. Eventually, Susan chose to describe Bryson's diagnosis as "multiple handicaps" on the application, a decision aimed at maximizing the available services.

Seeing these words written down triggered a mix of emotions. While the idea of "labeling" my son brought a sense of heaviness and heartache, there was also a profound relief that he hadn't been assigned a potentially limiting label. Navigating the delicate balance between these conflicting thoughts left me feeling confused, saddened, and apprehensive about what lay ahead for my son.

What significance lies in a name, and what weight does a label carry? For years, I struggled with how to characterize Bryson. Primarily, I referred to him as having special needs- a seemingly safe term. My rationalization was that "Everyone in the world has some kind of special need, right?" That term doesn't sound harsh. In my upbringing, "handicapped" was the prevalent term, still evident in "handicapped" parking spaces. Today's experts advocate abandoning the term special needs and substituting it with "disabled." Another term, socially frowned upon but still utilized in the medical realm is "mentally retarded"

It wasn't until I applied for government assistance that the doctor, filling out the paperwork, wrote Bryson's primary diagnosis as MR. Initially puzzled, it dawned on me- it was the label that no mother wishes for her child, but medically, that's what he was. The truth was undeniable, substantiated by his IQ test falling within that range. "Special needs" sounds kinder, perhaps less painful. Yet, as the scripture says in John 8:32, "And you will know the **truth**, and the **truth** will **set** you **free**." (emphasis added)

In Bryson's early years, I found myself unprepared for the freedom that the verse alluded to. Instead, I chose denial as my shield. Why wasn't I ready for that freedom? Denial seemed gentler and more manageable. The reality of Bryson's situation was fought with pain; it forced me to confront truths that I wasn't ready to face, such as the idea that God hadn't answered my childhood prayer about not wanting a handicapped child. If He didn't hear my prayer, could I trust Him? As the saying goes, "Admitting is the first step to healing," I was a long way from acknowledging the truth and oblivious to the need for healing.

The label "multiple handicaps" intended to keep options open for Bryson ironically became a hindrance. Bryson's labels were multiple handicaps and moderate learning disabilities. Honestly, I never quite knew how to explain Bryson's situation. My usual explanation was, "Bryson had a stroke in utero and that made him with a right-side hemiplegia (weakness), Cerebral Palsy, and he has seizures and learning disabilities." Occasionally, for dramatic effect, I'd mention that he was missing 76% of the left side of his brain.

My explanation sufficed for years. However, having a clearer diagnosis/label for Bryson could have helped with receiving services, and I could have had fewer clashes with the system instead of the "multiple handicaps" on his IEP throughout his school career. I recall times when I yearned for a label for him. There were support groups for Autism, Down Syndrome, and other syndromes. My child didn't fit neatly into any of these categories.

I felt isolated, raising a child with multiple handicaps, seemingly without a fitting place to find the support I needed.

What is an IEP? It stands for Individualized Education Program. The online definition "is a program tailored to meet the individual needs of students with disabilities. The program is written in collaboration between a child's school district, their parent or guardian, and sometimes, the student. The document outlines the special educational needs based on the student's identified disability. It outlines educational goals, and any specialist services they may need to meet those goals."[11] Now that you have read the online definition, allow me to paint a more vivid picture from my experiences:

An IEP meeting unfolds as parents gather around the long, polished conference table, flanked by 8-10 individuals "professionals" in their respective fields. Here, they dissect every facet of your child's strengths and challenges, proposing services the school can offer. The discussion navigates through an array of tests, reports, and medical information. The "professionals" seem knowledgeable about everything regarding your child and what is best for your child. The atmosphere is charged with tension. As a parent, you find yourself swimming in a wave of emotions you didn't realize were there: grief, exhaustion from the onslaught of information, and astonishment at how much others seem to know about your child while simultaneously feeling that they don't truly understand them at all. You ache to shout out your child's strengths, to champion them amidst the sea of concerns. Internally, you battle to hold back tears, to maintain a facade of strength. Yet, in it all, you're tasked with making decisions that will shape your child's future, grappling with the pressing question: do they truly understand and care for your child's well-being?

Bryson was my first child entering the educational world. I found myself lacking confidence in my ability to make the right decision. I felt inferior, uneducated in this unfamiliar territory, and the fear of making a mistake loomed large in my mind. Similar to my approach during his earlier medical experiences, I placed my trust in the educational experts. Advocating for Bryson's educational rights began with minor conflicts, but as the years passed, the stark reality became undeniable; the older he grew, the more formidable the battles became, and it fell upon me to champion his cause.

The first conflict I had to engage in was the desire to place Bryson in a Montessori preschool instead of the regular special education preschool REACH. I had researched the benefits of Montessori and, in my motherly attempt to give Bryson all the best opportunities available for him, I wanted him in a Montessori classroom. Bryson initially began his educational journey at the REACH preschool. During this time, I engaged in numerous meetings with the special education administration to navigate how this transition would unfold. REACH was state-funded and Montessori was private pay. I was requesting that the state cover the private pay costs. Through persistent advocacy, we eventually received the gratifying news that the state would cover Bryson's expenses to attend Montessori. Bryson continued to receive his therapies from special education therapists while attending Montessori, and his REACH teacher remained his designated instructor on his IEP.

During that particular season of life, I wasn't fully aware of the profound motivations guiding my decisions. In retrospect, my fervent desire for him to be among "normal" peers, as opposed to exclusively with other special education children, became evident from the outset of his educational journey. I was advocating for inclusion rather than segregation. I believed that bringing children of all abilities together could celebrate the beauty found in their differences.

Bryson excelled in the Montessori classroom. A Montessori classroom is a carefully curated environment designed to foster independence, curiosity, and a love for learning. One of their fundamental principles gives children the freedom to choose their activities. Within this setting, Bryson was able to select materials that aligned with his developmental needs. Without the ability to walk, Bryson maneuvered around the classroom scooting on his butt, pushing off with his strong left hand. His lack of vocabulary didn't hinder him in his learning, and the teachers provided guidance to discover creative ways for him to communicate.

This peaceful and simple environment helped Bryson gain confidence in himself, not focusing on his differences.

The normal transition for special education students was to attend the large city school that housed a functional skills classroom. After attending Montessori for three years, I was reluctant about the next phase of Bryson's education. He had recently mastered the art of walking, and that opened up a new freedom for him, but he still lacked vocabulary and had all of his medical issues. As Bryson grew older, I saw the gap of differences growing larger; opting for a functional skills classroom seemed like the most straightforward decision.

Bryson attended the functional skills classroom for kindergarten, 1st, 2nd, and 3rd grade. He had a wonderful teacher, Donna, and great helpers in the classroom. But, in the beginning of his third-grade year, Bryson started showing behaviors that were not normal for him. The classroom housed students of various ages, and he had finally discovered the world of words. One afternoon, he arrived home and confidently told me a word that was not in our family's vocabulary and not appropriate for a child or anyone. At that moment, Brad and I realized that this environment wasn't suitable for Bryson. He needed peers who could inspire him and motivate him to progress.

During these years of Bryson in the functional skills classroom, our family had moved three miles into the county with the aspiration that our children could attend the school system from which I had graduated. Tyrell attended their elementary school, but Bryson was picked up by the special education bus and taken back into the city limits to his classroom. As we wrestled with the new behaviors Bryson was demonstrating, we realized that we moved to the country so that "ALL" of our children could attend the same school system.

I began inquiring about the possibility of enrolling Bryson in the elementary school within our district. During the initial meeting to discuss options, an obvious strain hung in the air. I was informed, somewhat abruptly, "Our school's population lacks a sufficient percentage of special education students to warrant our own program. That's why we buy seats at the larger school for children with similar needs." Departing from the meeting, I sensed a closed door, leaving me deflated and frustrated.

Sensing the door was closed for mainstreaming education in our school district, I started pursuing the idea of sending Bryson to a private school. Our neighbor and friend, Gail, employed by the local private school, was well acquainted with the special education system and she helped us flesh out the pros and cons of private school and the unique requirements that Bryson would need. There was always an underlying feeling of unrest and, after a late night discussion, Brad and I again declared this was not what we wanted for our family. We wanted our boys in the same school.

Gail suggested I go straight to the county's special education director. The director had a different viewpoint and told me, "Your son is welcome at Benton." I left the meeting feeling excited about the possibilities. Benton Elementary School was a 5-star school, and it prided itself on its high academic achievement. Bringing a student into the mix who didn't fit this pedigree was not on the school's radar. Inclusion was a largely unfamiliar word in the education world. Taking the words "Your son is welcome at Benton," I marched ahead to make the move from the functional skills special education classroom to mainstream education for Bryson.

The day arrived for Bryson's first IEP in mainstream education. My heart rate was elevated, my neck muscles tense as Brad and I entered the conference room. The conference room was bright from the overhead lights, a display of educational posters and bulletin boards reflecting the academic environment. A long, polished conference table took center stage. The room was familiar. I had entered this room before, but the last time, I was told my child wasn't a fit for their school.

The atmosphere was charged with tangible friction, and the conference table was already full with the principal, special education teacher, occupational, physical, speech therapist and several representatives from ECSEC, the county's special education department. Brad and I, accompanied by Gail as our advocate, filled the last empty seats. Situations like this increased my insecurity, casting a shadow of doubt over my every move. I felt like I was facing a firing squad, the fear of judgment and scrutiny bearing down on me, even though not a word had been spoken. My lack of confidence loomed large, manifested by my sweaty palms. Despite the trembling fear of the little girl inside me, I knew I had to stand tall and fight for what was best for my son.

The meeting started out in normal IEP fashion: reviewing the previous IEP, his strengths and weaknesses, goals, his recent test results. However, as we transitioned to discussing the upcoming school year, an undeniable shift in the mood occurred. When I expressed a few aspirations for Bryson, the special education teacher responded promptly with a dismissive tone, stating, "I don't do that in 3rd grade." This set the tone for the next minutes, with our desires met by school rejections or excuses for their inability to fulfill them. My frustration mounted steadily.

As the meeting showed signs that a resolution wasn't going to be met, the principal interjected, "We will do the best that we can. If we can use the illustration that we are a general practitioner not a specialist, we will do the best we can, but sometimes you need a specialist." These words proved to be the tipping point. As a mother, I interpreted them as implying, "Your kid isn't good enough for this top-rated school." Hurt and anger surged within me. I raised my voice, sitting up, locking eyes with the principal, tears falling, and uttered, "What do you want me to do- just throw my child away?" The agony of realizing your child was not wanted cut deep. It pierced the already battered edges of my heart. All I sought was the best place for my son, yet he was UNWANTED.

Leaving the school building, I felt the weight of tension and emotions in my neck and shoulders, a physical manifestation of the turmoil from the meeting. My heart was heavy, longing to retreat home, bury my head under a pillow, and release the tears building inside. The battle wasn't just for my son's education; it was grappling with the sorrow of his lack of acceptance, grieving the differences that set him apart, and wrestling with the anger toward an education system that seemed to only value academic achievement over his individuality. I could sense Brad's own struggle with emotions mirroring mine. Gail's kind reassurance offered a glimmer of hope amidst the turmoil, promising to stand by our side, fight alongside us, and ultimately secure Bryson's place at Benton.

In the following weeks, we met with Gail to explore the various avenues available to us in pursuit of our objective, a place at Benton. Through these discussions, we made the decision to shift Bryson off the diploma pathway. This decision spared him from undergoing the challenging academic tests mandated by the state for grade progression. By doing so, his scores wouldn't be recorded, alleviating any potential impact on the school's reputation.

The decision to transition Bryson off the diploma track hit me hard. Academics had been a cornerstone of my own sense of worth, and removing this pathway from him felt like ripping off a bandage. While I knew it was the best choice for Bryson, it felt like a form of death- a death of the path I had envisioned and hoped for him. Grief, combined with a mix of other emotions, played havoc with me over this decision. Additionally, we opted for him to repeat 3rd grade, hoping that this decision would provide a more conducive environment with his individual needs and learning pace.

Through persistent advocacy and a few more tension-filled meetings, offering our compromises and taking their compromise for a shared paraprofessional, instead of a one on one paraprofessional, we managed to reach a consensus with the school. Paraprofessionals, para for short, play a crucial role in supporting the educational and developmental needs of students with disabilities. Paraprofessionals provide instructional, behavioral, and other support to students in and outside the classroom under the direction of a certified teacher.[12]

The initial months proved academically challenging, with Gail, my advocate, and I offering suggestions to better meet Bryson's needs. However, we encountered resistance, met with statements like "We don't have time, we can't do that here, that can't work." The overall response from the special education staff was, "We shouldn't worry about Bryson's academics; he is getting social and life skills." Again, my heart sensed that Bryson was overlooked and unwanted.

Undeterred, I took action by sending a letter to the school principal, asking for necessary accommodations. Slowly, throughout the first year, we managed to establish appropriate goals, and Bryson began receiving the services he needed. Despite all the academic hurdles, Bryson thrived socially and emotionally. His teachers embraced him and made him feel like an integral part of the class. His classmates accepted him, and he experienced newfound happiness. Eventually, Bryson secured a full-time one-on-one para to support him. The fight for his placement at Benton was hard, marked by moments of anger and sadness, but it proved worthwhile as Bryson found his place and truly felt like he belonged.

After completing four years at elementary school, the transition from 6th to 7th grade presented the next challenge. Once again, our smaller country school seemed unprepared to accommodate Bryson. Despite his remarkable progress in elementary school, they viewed him as fitting into a functional skills classroom back at the larger city school we had left four years before. Additionally, the smaller school lacked full-time one-on-one paras in the junior high and high school settings, which I deemed essential.

Again, I was back in a conference room, just as described before. The only difference this time, it was at the Junior/Senior high school. This time in addition to the special education representatives normally at an IEP, we now had staff from the elementary school and the Junior/Senior high school. Sitting across from Brad and me at the large oblong table was the principal of Benton, the same principal I had confronted four years prior, asking him, "What do you want me to do, just throw my child away?" This time, however, there was no fear or anger between us. He was now an ally. Over the years, we had cultivated a positive relationship.

During the meeting, the principal and other elementary staff spoke about Bryson's significant positive impact on the school community. They acknowledged that while Bryson may not have met all the academic benchmarks, his social engagement, enthusiasm, and active participation in various activities, especially sports, had made him well-known and well-liked among his peers. It was a remarkable turn-around, illustrating how perceptions can change when given a chance. Bryson brought a valuable sense of knowledge and social awareness to his peers, fostering a deeper understanding of the disability world.

As I listened to the praise from the Benton staff, finally hearing positive affirmations about Bryson, I felt a heaviness lift from my mama heart. For once, I heard that he was appreciated for who he was. It was as if I had been holding my breath, and I could now release it, allowing myself to rest.

While the junior high staff did not express a lack of desire for Bryson, it became clear that logistical challenges stood in the way. They explained that they lacked one-on-one paras at this level, and their special education was small. Consequently, Bryson once again qualified for the functional skills classroom rather than a mainstream path.

By this point, I was well aware of my rights, and I approached the situation with confidence, articulating clearly what I believed was best for my son. I knew that if they resisted, I had the legal backing of IDEA to support my position.

IDEA (Individuals with disabilities education act) is an act that was originally called the Education for All Handicapped Children Act when it started in 1975. It then was reauthorized and renamed in 1990. IDEA covers children from birth through high school graduation or age 21, whichever comes first. The act has two primary responsibilities on states and public schools: to provide a free appropriate public education to children with disabilities and to ensure that these children learn in the least restrictive environment, meaning they should be educated alongside their non-disabled peers as much as possible.[13]

As I left the IEP meeting at Fairfield, emotions bubbled beneath the surface, but this time, they weren't tears of grief or anger. Instead, these were tears of pride and relief. I had advocated tirelessly for Bryson, and the efforts had paid off. Fairfield had agreed to provide Bryson with a one-on-one paraprofessional, and we had reached an agreement on his daily schedule. While he would be in a special education classroom for English and Math, for the rest of his classes, he would join the regular classroom with his para.

I felt the sense of triumph knowing that I had secured a place where I believed that Bryson could thrive. It was a moment of validation, affirming that my advocacy had made a real difference in Bryson's life.

The following six years were not free from academic conflicts. The special education department exhibited a notable lack of comprehension regarding essential requirements of the IEP and struggled with consistent follow-through. Once again, I found myself in a crucial meeting, this time convened at the administration building. Seated around a small round table, the superintendent of the school system and the special education coordinator joined me. With assertiveness, I brought to their attention the school's failure to adhere to Bryson's IEP. Emphasizing my right to pursue legal action, I emphasized the crucial importance of adhering to the goals outlined in Bryson's IEP to support him in achieving his full potential. The superintendent acknowledged the necessity for the school to improve its adherence to the IEP, recognizing its pivotal role in Bryson's educational journey. I experienced a sense of being heard that day. Striking the delicate balance between advocating fiercely for his rights and understanding the need for a tactful and strategic approach posed an ongoing challenge.

I crafted a personal motto: "Fight with all your might, fight with grace and truth, but don't burn bridges." I understood that in following this principle, I could achieve more than if I resorted to words of judgment and hostility.

I developed a relationship with the special education administrators and staff, they all knew my name and understood my unwavering commitment to fight for my son. While some of my actions and words were assertive and firm, I hoped they perceived that my ultimate goal was to secure the best possible outcome for Bryson. Over the years, I received phone calls from the school, each time causing a momentary flutter in my heart, my mind would immediately think the worst, however, more often than not, I would hear, "Hi, don't worry, everything is fine… we just need…."

Paraprofessionals are often unsung heroes in the special education realm. Over Bryson's decade in the mainstream school system, he was blessed to have three amazing and exceptional paraprofessionals. In the classroom, Bryson's paras modified and adapted instructional materials to meet his unique needs. They helped teach him how to navigate social situations, also aiding him during lunchtime and offering support in daily tasks; their impact extended far beyond the classroom.

This position doesn't compensate enough for a person to live on. A good para, instead, must have a genuine desire and passion for the job and the students they work with. Bryson's paras went above and beyond, not just fulfilling their roles but actively caring for him and creating an environment where he could succeed. Their love for Bryson was evident in their commitment to pushing him to achieve his best.

Bryson's classmates played a pivotal role in making him feel included, treating him with kindness and making him feel seen and normal. Whether it was chatting about his favorite sports teams, school, or his insights on coaching, they embraced him. His role as football and eventually, basketball manager, solidified his place among his peers, as they watched out for him and actively involved him. At school events or in the community, the recognition and friendly greetings directed at Bryson felt like a reward for the persistent advocacy efforts I had undertaken to ensure he found his place.

A special bond with Mr. Fritz, a physical education teacher and assistant sports director, led to Bryson interning in the PE classroom during his last few years of school. Mr. Fritz often told me, "Bryson could run the class." This experience boosted Bryson's self-esteem and worth. His internships extended to the front office during his senior year where he took on various tasks, highlighting his capabilities. The office staff did an excellent job of spoiling Bryson during his senior year. The two school nurses who worked with him went above and beyond, providing care and support beyond their job descriptions. Their dedication ensured I could trust Bryson's safety during the 8 hours he spent away from my care every day. While Bryson may not have been invited to activities beyond the school day and sports, the love and care he received during these eight hours were immeasurable. It was a testament to the supportive community that embraced him within the school walls.

The day Bryson walked across the graduation stage to receive his certificate of completion marked a moment of reflection and happiness. His journey, though different, echoes some parallels with my own. I had placed my value on academics, striving for perfection while struggling with my confidence in the social world. The pivotal decision to transition Bryson off the diploma track in 3rd grade was not taken lightly; it meant removing education as a marker of his worth. Bryson not only adapted but thrived in his unique educational setting. His physical disability, distinct educational materials, and the constant presence of his para did not hinder him. Instead, he embraced his life and made the best of it.

In my readings through the years, God led me to find the book *Adam God's Beloved* by Henri J. M. Nouwen.[14] This poignant narrative unfolds Nouwen's sabbatical at L'Arche Daybreak Community, where he dedicated himself to serving a severely disabled man named Adam. As I delved into the pages of the book, tears welled up as I witnessed how God utilized Adam to impart, stir, and instruct a Dutch Priest, ultimately deepening his understanding of Jesus, all without Adam uttering a single word. Nouwen reflected, "Indeed, not only did I come to know more about God by caring for Adam, but also Adam helped me, by his life, to discover and rediscover the Spirit of Jesus alive in my own 'poorness of spirit.'

Whenever the insecurities of my youth surfaced. I would return to the truths unveiled in the book. Through this, I recognized how God, in His wisdom, used Bryson to impact numerous lessons simply by being Bryson – a testament to the transformative power of God and His grace.

The quote at the beginning of this chapter resonates deeply. The last words sum it up well.

Our toil will be a thousand times repaid, not perhaps by the successful result of a competitive examination, but by the useful, loving, and healthy life.

CHAPTER 7
Another Life Changing Moment

"You can do more than pray, after you have prayed. But you cannot do more than pray until you have prayed."
S.D. Gordon[15]

"What are we going to do for spring break this year?" Ty asked me shortly after getting off the bus from school. I didn't like this question. We weren't the family that made big trips during this time, and we weren't the ones who went to Florida every year. Each year, we struggled to decide what we would do that was special with the boys during their week off school. I knew that Ty had been hearing vacation plans from his friends and he wanted to do something cool also. Brad and I discussed it later in the evening and knew that we needed to plan at least a few days of break. April in Indiana is always a hit-and-miss with the weather. It could feel totally like winter, or it could have a tinge of spring in the air. Our options were small if we wanted to stay close to home.

It was a hazy, chilly Friday afternoon as we headed in our light green minivan to Kalamazoo, Michigan, a one and ¼ hour drive from home. The boys were excited to be staying in a hotel for a couple of nights and away from home. With a family of 5, Kaden, as the baby, always had to sleep on the floor. Removing the spare blanket from the dresser and using a blanket that we had brought, we made him a nest beside our bed. At the age of 10 and 8, Bryson and Ty didn't mind sleeping in the same bed, but that attitude changed only a few years later.

Hotel sleeping isn't usually the best, and we were up early. The dining area of the Holiday Inn had tall ceilings and large glass windows. I looked out the frosted windows and could see the traffic whizzing by on the freeway. We sat at a large round table and ordered our breakfast. As we ate, I noticed Bryson had drunk several glasses of water, which amazed me because he wasn't a water guy. After we finished breakfast, we had to waste some time before the Kalamazoo Air Zoo opened, and we continued to sit around the table. The boys were restless. Bryson complained that he was thirsty. I questioned him, but he insisted that he needed something else to drink. Breakfast hours had ended, and so Brad left the room to find a vending machine. He returned with a can of Pepsi. Bryson guzzled it down. Shortly after, he needed to use the restroom, and Brad left with him.

"What is going on with Bryson?" I asked Brad as we headed out across the parking lot of the hotel to our van. I was irritated. This wasn't normal for him, and I didn't like this extra distraction. Brad echoed my sentiments, but we didn't have an answer.

As we walked around the Air Zoo, Ty and Kaden engaged in the activities available. Bryson stayed aloof and kept asking for something to drink. With frustration, we gave him more to drink and took turns taking him to the restroom.

Bryson lacked a large vocabulary and had a tough time telling us what he was experiencing. We tried to keep a light attitude to not ruin the "fun" we were all trying to have as a family.

Another Life Changing Moment

In the evening, we attended the Kalamazoo K Wings hockey game, the last one of the season for them. Our tickets were in the east corner of the arena, nestled in the middle of the aisle. Brad, an avid hockey fan, was intensely concentrating on the game, so my role was to take Bryson back and forth to the restroom. As I periodically glanced over at Bryson, my mind raced with thoughts, trying to decipher what could be bothering him. Yet, I couldn't shake off my own agitation. I found myself tapping my foot and shifting restlessly in my seat, my stomach knotting with nervousness. I knew that if I didn't respond immediately when he asked to go to the restroom, we would have trouble.

Our return trip home was uneventful, and Bryson seemed to have leveled out with his thirst and need to urinate. I communicated with his para at school on Monday morning about the weekend for her to be aware if Bryson displayed any of these symptoms at school. I didn't hear anything from the school on Monday, but, Tuesday afternoon, I received a call from the school nurse. She informed me that Bryson had wet his pants. Hanging up the phone after speaking with the nurse, confusion washed over me like a wave, leaving me feeling disoriented. This was uncharted territory, a situation he had never encountered before. A sense of heaviness settled on my chest, making each breath feel uncertain. I noticed my hands were involuntarily clenching into fists.

Recollections of the recent spring break week flooded my mind- the instances of Bryson's increased thirst and frequent urination. I had desperately hoped it was merely a passing illness, nothing more. Without hesitation, I drove to Fairfield to pick up Bryson.

Upon seeing Bryson's downcast and quiet demeanor, I sensed the confusion that mirrored my own. He had never wet his pants before, and now both of us were grappling with what was wrong. Upon arriving home, I immediately contacted our family physician, scheduling an appointment for Thursday afternoon.

Bryson remained unusually quiet on Wednesday. I opted to keep him at home, uncertain of what was unfolding. He didn't feel sick, just frequent urges to urinate. My body felt drained, aching for rest, yet I forced myself to stay occupied with mundane tasks, desperate to prevent my mind from wandering into realms of fear and anxiety.

Through the numerous trials we had faced with Bryson, I had come to trust my mama heart implicitly. I had learned to heed the whispers of concern that echoed in my mind; after all, I knew my child better than anyone else. Deep within my gut, I sensed an unsettling certainty that something was seriously wrong, but I didn't want to think about what could be looming ahead. Throughout the day, I cried out to God, sometimes in silent desperation, other times in audible pleas, begging for reassurance: "God, please, nothing else, don't let it be anything serious."

However, no amount of prayer or distraction could ease the gnawing unease that gripped my body and heart as I awaited the upcoming doctor's appointment.

As I drove Bryson to the doctor's appointment, I felt the tension in my neck and shoulders, and my mind was in a fog. Slowly, we walked into the waiting room of the doctor's office. I told Bryson to sit in one of the black chairs in the middle of the room. I approached the check-in window. The nurse knew me well, as we were frequent flyers at the office. My hands were dry, and I rubbed my hands together in a nervous gesture. The 15-minute wait seemed like a day. Bryson was quiet. He, too, had experienced so many medical scares that I'm sure he felt something. My heart broke for my 10-year-old son. Life had not been easy for him.

Weight, height, blood pressure, and pulse were taken by the nurse, and we waited for the doctor to arrive. As I assisted Bryson onto the examination table, I noticed the way he grabbed my hand and leaned on me for support. The room had a comforting ambiance, and I took a seat near the window. The room was adorned with colorful kid pictures, ranging from whimsical drawings of animals to vibrant depictions of landscapes. The space was decorated to feel warm and welcoming, but my heart didn't feel the warmth, and the unknown left a chill in the air. The doctor, tall and stocky, with light brown hair and a subtle hint of gray, entered the room. We quickly engaged in conversation regarding Bryson's symptoms and events that had transpired over the past week. With a warm and approachable demeanor, he asked, "Have you taken Bryson's blood sugar?" Blood sugar. This had never entered my mind. "No, I never thought about that," I replied with fear in my voice. The doctor immediately requested the nurse to come in and administer the test. The nurse entered, poked his right middle finger, and left the room, the doctor following behind her. Bryson and I sat in silence for the next few minutes until the doctor returned. His face showed anxiety and tension.

"Bryson's blood sugar is almost 600," the doctor said. "We need to get him to the hospital ASAP." Wait, what? "What are you saying?" I uttered. "It appears that Bryson had Juvenile Diabetes, Type 1 Diabetes," the doctor replied. "I need to find a pediatric endocrinologist that can see him immediately. I will go and make some phone calls." As he left, I sensed his urgency and his concern. What is Type 1? I don't know anything about this. I picked up my phone and called Brad. Numbness washed over me, and I felt as if I was teetering on the edge of disbelief. With a trembling voice, I stammered out to Brad, "The doctor says Bryson has Type 1 Diabetes, and we have to go to a hospital immediately." The words sounded hollow and surreal as they left my lips. Hastily, I instructed Brad to stay put until I had more information, just as the doctor reentered the room and spoke, "Dr. Thomas at Ft Wayne Lutheran Children's Hospital will see him. Do you want him to go by ambulance, or will you take him? He needs to get there in the next few hours."

My heart raced as memories of previous ambulance rides for Bryson flooded my mind – the urgency, the fear. I informed the doctor that I needed to consult Brad to determine the best course of action. Following our discussion, we decided on transporting him ourselves to the hospital located one and ¼ hours away. As we remained seated in the exam room, the overwhelming urge to collapse and release a torrent of tears washed over me. Every fiber of my being longed to scream a resounding "NO!" My body felt paralyzed. But I knew I couldn't succumb to those emotions, not here, not in front of Bryson. I had to find the courage to summon every ounce of strength to maintain my composure. I needed to be strong, to ease Bryson's confusion and fear.

I knew that Bryson didn't understand the magnitude of the crisis at hand and the need for another hospital visit. He didn't feel sick. "Bryson, because you have been very thirsty and peeing often, we need to see a new doctor," I explained to him. Familiar with doctors and hospitals, Bryson accepted the words I said and just quietly nodded his head. I swiftly transitioned into crisis mode, my emotions in check and forged ahead to ensure the necessary actions were taken care of.

I called my mom on the drive home from the doctor to ask her to come stay with Ty and Kaden. Feeling disconnected, as if I was floating, I was grateful that God got me home safely. *What did I need to pack, and how long would I be gone?* I didn't know. Brad had arrived home from work, and we hurried to pack a few things into the suitcase. I sat in the back with Bryson, and we brought along an ice cream bucket in case Bryson had to pee while we were driving.

Coming down Highway 69, heading south out of Ft Wayne, my stomach was churning as we got closer. I had flashbacks to other trips we had taken to the hospital with him, RSV, dehydration, respiratory distress, and appendicitis. Each of these experiences had left a scar in my heart and mind. I had been to many other hospitals, but I had not been to Lutheran. Brad had driven with a sense of urgency, trying not to speed. It was knowing that this was an urgent matter but not understanding the magnitude of what was going on.

We entered through the emergency area, and I told them what we were there for. They had been informed that we would be arriving, and we were escorted up several floors. There were stickers on the walls, and the hallway was dimly lit. We passed door after door; each door stained a deep mahogany tone with a window. The nurse led us to the end of the hallway, and we were invited into Bryson's room and to make ourselves at home. It was early evening by the time we arrived, so not much was going to happen. The nurse arrived and administered an insulin shot into Bryson's stomach for the first time. We were told we would be given an orientation the next day to teach us all about Type 1 Diabetes.

Brad and I sat on the two hard wooden chairs in Bryson's room as he sat on the hospital bed. His room had the usual hospital curtains of pink, purple, yellow, and red stripes. The walls had a border of cartoon children around the middle of the room. It was supposed to be cheery, but there was no cheer in the room. As we sat there observing our surroundings, the future looked scary. What new challenges would this bring to Bryson's already challenged life?

Before Brad left for the night, the nurse asked us to help administer Bryson's insulin shot. I wasn't ready to do it. After the nurse calculated the correct dose and drew up the insulin, she gave the needle to Brad. Brad sat across from Bryson, who was wearing his favorite PJs at the time, pants sporting a maple leaf with the word Canada written all over them. He gave Bryson his first shot from his parents. I stood off to the side, trying to grasp the fact that this would be what we would have to do forever, unless God performed a miracle. Bryson didn't even flinch. He didn't question. He just watched as the needle went into his stomach. I felt nauseous.

As I settled into the uncomfortable hospital chair-turned-sofa bed in Bryson's room for the night, I laid there, and my mind wouldn't settle. I journaled....

Bryson has Juvenile Diabetes, what is next? God, are you there? I know you are faithful; I know that you will provide, and I want to trust you. I know I'm strong, but God I just want to cry out, I'm mad and I am feeling sorry for myself. God, why Bryson, he has had so many challenges already, and he doesn't understand the extent of what is going on. God, I am going to have to do all the work. Brad helps but I DO everything. I want to do it with joy, my heart loves Bryson, but I want to be selfish, I want to scream, I don't want this responsibility. How do I handle this? How do I instruct my mother, who is my primary caregiver, to do this? How do I teach the nurse at school, I'm struggling with the school system already and now add this. My stomach hurts, my heart aches, I want to talk to someone. Who do I talk to, what do I say? I am supposed to be strong, I'm supposed to just go on, because God is faithful, but WHY God WHY!

As I lamented to God that night, I drifted in and out of sleep. The nurses floated in and out of the room all night, checking Bryson's vitals and his blood sugar numbers. Suddenly, I was awakened by the room shaking. It lasted about 15 seconds. I was puzzled. I got up and surveyed the room; nothing seemed amiss and Bryson was thankfully still asleep. I didn't know what to make of it so I lay back down, but my sleep was totally gone. My body, mind, and spirit were exhausted. I knew that the day ahead was going to be full of lots of information. *God, give me the strength for today.*

Mid-morning, Brad arrived back to the room, exhausted from the long drive, lack of sleep, and stress. Shortly after his arrival, the door to Bryson's room opened, and a nurse walked in wearing her royal blue smock sporting bright yellow stars, moon, and cheerful characters. Her shirt matched her cheerful spirit. She gave Bryson a high five and introduced herself as Cindy, the diabetes educator for Dr. Thomas. Cindy became a fast friend who always had a cheerful spirit each time we went to the Dr's office over the next years.

"Did you feel a shaking during the night?" Cindy asked. "Yes," I replied. Cindy went on to explain that Ft. Wayne had experienced a 5.4 magnitude earthquake around 5:38 am. Looking back, the earthquake was so fitting, as the earth trembled and shook, so did our lives. This diagnosis was life changing and shattering.

Brad and I received a five-hour crash course in diabetes care. We learned all about carbs, ratios, and formulas. We learned that Bryson would need four shots of insulin a day. All food that entered his body would have to be calculated, and he would have to receive a shot of insulin based on the ratio set for him. She gave us paper after paper of instructions for daily management. As we were nearing the end of the orientation, Cindy said, "The last thing we have to do is for mom and dad to give themselves a shot of water into their stomachs so that they understand how it feels for Bryson to get his shot." *What, I have to poke myself with a needle?* My mind was worn out, I was exhausted, and now I had to administer a needle to my stomach. Brad went first. Bryson, wearing his Benton Elementary t-shirt, stood beside Brad and watched him. Then he turned around as I sat on the edge of his bed, covered with a light blue blanket, and I stuck myself with a needle. It was all surreal.

Shortly after, we packed up our bags, and what felt like tons of paperwork and headed home. Fear loomed large. Just like that, I was now responsible for making sure my son stayed alive. My mind raced… I could kill him by not administering the right amount of insulin… he could die in his sleep if his blood sugar went too low while he slept…will I ever sleep again, free from the burdens of fear and worry?

This pivotal moment, a life-altering event, changed everything. I was not only administering seizure medication twice a day, but my responsibilities also mushroomed into a complex ritual of carb counting, calculating insulin ratios, and administering insulin shots, a full-time job. Thankfully, the school nurse proved to be an invaluable ally, and Bryson, resilient in the face of adversity, embraced yet another challenge with unwavering acceptance.

I wanted to emulate Bryson's attitude, yet my heart shattered, and my body, weary, struggled to hold up to this new challenge. In many ways, I felt like I was losing my identity, merely going through the motions of life. The diagnosis felt like the final blow, extinguishing any chance for relief or a break. Holding Bryson's life in my hands, I couldn't escape the weight of responsibility. They say that caring for someone with Type 1 Diabetes who can't manage themselves, feels like bearing the burden personally. Suddenly, my identity became Diabetes.

Inside, I harbored unspoken anger. I hadn't discovered the freedom to express it. I struggled to even name the raw, ugly emotion that seemed to fester within me. It felt unjust- Bryson already faced so many challenges, why did God have to add this life-altering event to the mix? My relationship with God felt strained and forced. I went through the motions of devotions and prayers out of a sense of obligation rather than genuine love and connection.

Several years into our journey with Type 1, a moment of exhaustion prompted me to share on my Facebook page, "Today, I am tired of Bryson having Diabetes." The relentless management of fluctuating blood sugar levels, the constant responsibilities, and the worry had left me thoroughly depleted. As I reflected on my emotions following this revelation, it brought to mind a poignant conversation with Bryson.

While driving home from town one afternoon, I mentioned the topic with him, "Bryson, we are going to start you on an insulin pump. I know you don't understand what it will do. It will be helpful because we won't have to give you four shots of insulin a day. The pump will give it to you." Bryson sat silently beside me for a few minutes, then courageously expressed his thoughts. "I wish I wouldn't have Diabetes anymore. I wish Duke would take my Diabetes." (Duke was Bryson's endearing nickname for his cousin, Jennilee, as he struggled with pronouncing her name.)

His words struck a deep chord within me, stirring tears in my eyes. As a mother, confronted with such a heartfelt statement, I longed to rid him of his burden with Diabetes. "Bryson, I wish I could take it away too, but remember God will help you through it," was all I could manage, the weight of reality too heavy. During our continued drive, I contemplated why he chose Duke to bear his wish. Bryson and Duke's relationship, the unconditional love, closeness, safety, and genuine care that Bryson felt from their connection, in Bryson's child-like heart, he entrusted her with his life, believing that she would always be there to love and nurture him.

The profound truth embedded in that conversation, a mantra I've repeated throughout the years, was the assurance I shared with Bryson that day – God would help him through it. This realization mirrored what my loving Heavenly Father desired from me. He beckoned me to approach Him and utter, "God, I don't want Diabetes anymore. I want you to take it from me." His desire was for an unconditional, close, safe, and loving relationship with me, urging me to trust Him with my life and to seek Him in every moment – daily, hourly, and every single minute. His commitment was steadfast; he will always be there for me, shouldering the burdens and responsibilities, whether it be the role of a mother or whatever struggle I may face.

In that moment of weariness, my cry transformed into a plea "Lord, when weariness overwhelms me, help me to claim Your Word and to find rest in Your presence, knowing that You are there and will provide everything I need."

> **Then Jesus said, "come to me, all of you who are weary and carry heavy burdens, I will give you rest. Take my yoke upon you. Let me teach you, because I am humble and gentle at heart, and you will find rest for your souls. For my yoke is easy to bear, and the burden I give you is light."**
> **Matthew 28-30**

CHAPTER 8

The Divine Calling that Broke Me

> "When we respond in obedience, however difficult it may seem, it is always for our benefit, because God is for us and not against us. Obedience to God is the key to a life full of love, joy, peace, hope, progress, success, blessing, abundance, and prosperity. Obedience is actually very simple; it's just not easy."
> Christine Caine[16]

While Bryson's care was a significant part of my life, I engaged in various other activities. I found fulfillment as I continued to work in our family construction and lumberyard business, dedicating at least one day a week, and occasionally more as demands required. Beyond the business realm, I immersed myself in women's ministry and discipleship classes within the church, actively participating in small groups. My vision extended beyond the church, envisioning a women's ministry outside traditional church settings. My dreams were grand, prompting me to hire the help of a life coach to navigate and actualize my dreams and goals. Although I found these sessions enriching and experienced personal growth, I remained stuck in the pursuit of my goals. Finally, my life coach gave me a gentle nudge: "I think you need to start looking back at your past. You can't move forward until you have found the healing you need."

This crucial advice led me to engage in inner healing work, confronting and addressing past issues. Intrigued by the concept of life coaching, I devoted five months in 2011 to online classes, earning certification in Hope Coaching, Spiritual Formation, and Stress Management. The thrill of receiving my Life Coach certificate was energizing.

However, health challenges emerged in 2012, suffering from continual aches and pains all over my body. I didn't find answers in the medical system. Through self-diagnosis via internet research, I labeled my condition as Fibromyalgia. The responsibilities of managing Bryson's medical issues undoubtedly played a role in my health issues. Facing pain and exhaustion, I spent many afternoons on my couch, but I continued to fulfill my obligations, accepting these challenges as normal life.

In the summer of 2013, an amazing opportunity presented itself. The chance to go on a mission trip to Jamaica with family members. I eagerly anticipated this trip as a much-needed break from the ongoing demands of Bryson. It was an opportunity for me to step back and trust Brad and my mom to take over his care, knowing they would provide him with the same level of attention that I would. Accompanied by my second son Tyrell, we headed to Jamaica. This trip held a special significance as one of Brad's nieces had adopted a young boy from Jamaica. It marked a poignant return for him to his homeland and our team to serve in various children's homes across the island.

The mission trip proved to be impactable and challenging. Witnessing the emptiness in the children's eyes and their hunger for attention left a profound ache in my heart. The first home we visited had a tattered sign on the door, handwritten in green marker, "All the time, God is good!" It ripped at my soul. Here, orphaned and living in a shanty of dirt and metal, they clung to the truth of God's goodness. One particular visit to Windsor Lodge in Mandeville, a Salvation Army run home, left an impressionable mark. Our task that day was to paint the boy's dorm room, transforming it into a space for the girls. While we were painting, a young boy named Stevan expressed a desire to help. The other children wanted to hang all over us and play with our hair, but Stevan wanted to work. We affectionately dubbed him "Supervisor Stevan." He shared with us a notebook filled with precious songs and poems that he had written, showcasing a sweet and gentle disposition.

Evenings were marked by reflective debriefing in a circle, the air thick with humidity after frequent rain and the daytime temperature nearly unbearable. As we discussed our experience at Windsor, Stevan's caring heart and eagerness to assist lingered in our conversations. His sincerity touched me deeply.

Returning home, the trip's impact weighed heavily on my heart. The sheer number of children in need of a family, coupled with the hopelessness of their futures, left an unforgettable mark. The heartache of the orphan had become a tangible reality. From our discussions as a team, my desire to make a difference revolved around providing aid to older teen boys in acquiring job skills, and preventing them from turning to a life of crime or drugs upon leaving the children's homes at 18. Additionally, God impressed upon my heart the responsibility to pray for three teenage girls from Windsor.

My heart had been transformed by the mission trip, I had witnessed the challenges faced by the people of Jamaica, I gained a newfound perspective beyond the confines of my world filled with mothering three boys, Bryson's care, and my health. My eyes were opened to the hardships of the world. With my gaze directed outward, I found myself less preoccupied with my own personal struggles.

Persistent health issues continued to cast a shadow over my well-being after I returned from Jamaica. A ray of hope arrived in the form of a text introducing me to health products that held the promise of relief. Eager to reclaim my health, I started on these products. In tandem with the health products, I jumped on the exercise train. Joining a local gym, I discovered a love for the elliptical machine. This combination set me on a path toward weight loss and overall good health.

The world felt brighter and clearer, I felt *hope*. The certificate that stated I was now a life coach was tucked away in the cabinet in my office. I pondered the question, "What all do you have for me God in this next phase of life?"

On a typical, overcast Thursday morning in November, with my weekly goal of hitting the gym three days a week, I set off shortly after the boys left for school. I claimed my favorite elliptical machine, plugged in my headphones, and immersed myself in the workout routine, setting my time and speed. Across the room, a TV hung from the ceiling, and this morning, the NBC Today Show captured my attention, featuring a family sharing their adoption experience. Intrigued, I listened, the elliptical miles passed swiftly, and soon, I completed my workout and headed home.

Upon returning home, my routine led me straight to the shower, a sanctuary where my mind often found clarity amidst the four walls. As the water fell, my thoughts flowed freely. Then, a distinct voice cut through, "Lisa, he is your son; bring him home," accompanied by a vivid picture of Stevan in his red shirt. My body shook with the weight of those clear, audible words. Exiting the shower, the thoughts and shaking lingered. *Had I just heard God? What now?*

Perhaps an unconventional response, but in the intensity of the moment, I found myself at my computer after getting dressed. Without hesitation, I composed an email to my accountability group.

"Ladies, I am going crazy right now. I just had a crazy thought, or a God moment and I don't know what to do with it. I'm throwing out the fleece, I haven't even talked to Brad about it yet.... But I have to spill it to a neutral source...

This morning, I had been praying for some of the kids from Jamaica that I had met this summer like I do, nothing unusual happened. When I was working out at the gym, they had a segment on the Today show about adoption, great, made me teary but finished my workout. Came home and get into the shower and it was like bang... Stevan in the red shirt popped into my head.

He was an amazing young man, 11 years old, full of vision and love for Jesus. I had this retching in my heart, and it was like I heard, "He is your son; bring him home." I have no idea if he is even adoptable and as you can tell, I haven't even shared this with my husband. I never had any heart pulls this summer when I was there. What am I to do, friends?"

Immediately after hitting the send button to my friends, I replicated the message and forwarded it to my husband, Brad. Adding a crucial note at the end - "I will be in the office in 20 minutes to talk about it." Upon arriving and settling at his desk, I looked at Brad and posed the question, "What do you think?" In response, without hesitation, he shared an unexpected revelation.

"Lisa, last night when I was at my men's group, we were talking about purpose and God's calling in our lives. I shared with them about my restlessness, asking God what he wanted from me." Brad paused briefly, then continued with a chuckle, "I then told them we could adopt, but my wife is not very domestic." Brad and I laughed. It had always been a shared understanding between us. I didn't enjoy staying at home, gardening, and cooking.

However, in that moment, facing the call that had just been revealed to me, Brad looked at me and said, "I don't know how we can say NO to this call. I believe it says clearly in the Bible we are to care for orphans, and I believe you heard from God." Despite never having met Stevan, Brad's response was an unwavering – resounding YES. The commitment to embrace the call, uncharted and unconventional as it was, spoke volumes about Brad's faith and the shared understanding that this path was God-ordained. With a simple YES, the trajectory of our lives pivoted towards a journey of adoption, guided by a shared belief in God's plan.

An ironic twist was that adoption resonated closely within Brad's family; and while my heart had remained open to the idea, I was convinced that adoption wasn't my path. Frequently, I would be asked about the need for a girl, given our three boys. In response, I consistently said, "If I'm meant to adopt, it will be a direct word from God."

With a clear sense that God had spoken resonating deep within my heart, I wholeheartedly committed myself to this new task. Reflecting on it now, I realize that I was determined to follow God's call. Subconsciously, perhaps I yearned for something beyond the constant challenges of Bryson's care that always loomed over me. I neglected to pause and thoroughly examine the potential impact of taking on this adoption alongside the myriad responsibilities I was already juggling. Instead, I was captivated by the prospect of hope and the opportunity to make a positive difference. God told me Stevan was my son. I had to go get him.

In the days that followed, we shared "the call" with our sons, Bryson, Tyrell, and Kaden. Tyrell, having recently experienced Jamaica, was also deeply affected by the hardships he witnessed there. Meeting Stevan, he immediately saw the potential for making a difference and embraced the idea wholeheartedly. Kaden, at just ten years old, eagerly joined in, thrilled at the prospect of gaining another brother. Despite Bryson's slower processing speed and limited ability to fully express his thoughts, he sensed the enthusiasm in his brothers and gave his approval when asked if he would be okay with another brother.

In addition to discussing the decision among ourselves, we reached out to our close family and friends, seeking their prayers and support as we navigated this significant decision. Together, we fervently sought God's guidance. In this space of seeking, confirmation of the call continued to be heard.

Recognizing the practical steps needed, I reached out to Patrick, a Jamaican friend who had been a part of the mission team. His local connection became instrumental as I asked him to inquire about Stevan's availability for adoption. The wheels were set in motion, merging faith with tangible action. One week after I felt the call, Patrick confirmed that Stevan was adoptable.

Jamaican adoptions were handled directly by the government, not through adoption agencies like we have in the United States. The task to bring Stevan into our family was a daunting one, and it became profoundly personal to me, much like the approach I had taken with Bryson's medical, therapy, and education. With full determination, I threw myself wholeheartedly into the process. Over the next year, paperwork was completed, battles were fought, and numerous trips were made back and forth to Jamaica. There were moments of frustration, tears, and questioning. I cried out to God, "*Why does this have to be so hard, God? This was your idea.*" All we wanted was to bring this young boy home, to offer him the warmth of family and the love of God.

Amidst the hardships and questions, I held onto the belief that God had called us to bring Stevan into our home. The desire was beyond just providing a home, but to create a safe place for him to heal, discover his passions, and nurture his hopes for the future. I clung to the blessing of being a part of a divine plan that God had orchestrated. I desired this experience, though demanding, to grow, mold, and become an instrument of God's love.

I wanted to be the hands and feet of Jesus to those in need.

Nine months into the grueling process and shortly after a brief visit to Jamaica with my son Kaden to see Stevan, my exhaustion and frustration reached a breaking point. In the depth of my weariness and the relentless striving to bring Stevan home, doubt crept in. I questioned whether God truly cared. Confusion between the divine calling and the feeling of unanswered prayers, I was ready to walk away from my faith. Where was God in all of this? Why is this so hard?

Night after night, images of Stevan alone on his bunk bed haunted my thoughts, fueling a growing anger. Instead of turning that anger towards God, I pushed Him away, continuing to battle the system to bring Stevan home. Recognizing the need for more than just inner healing, I sought help from a professional therapist to navigate the emotional toll of this journey.

Thankfully, God intervened creatively by bringing a revival to our county in the spring of 2015, a year and three months after we had started the adoption process. This spiritual awakening became a soothing balm for my weary soul. Through powerful testimonies, miraculous stories, and the tangible movement of the Holy Spirit, my heart began to thaw. Trust in God was rebirthed, renewing my resolve to trust His divine plan. The revival breathed new life into my faith.

The long-awaited news arrived, signaling the completion of paperwork and the moment we could finally bring Stevan home. As we prepared for the trip to pick up Stevan, Brad and I struggled with the decision of whether to bring Bryson along with us. On one hand, we desired for it to be a whole family experience. However, considering all of Bryson's care needs, I realized that I wouldn't be able to devote my full attention to Stevan. I anticipated that this journey would be emotionally and physically draining, and I didn't want the additional responsibility and worry for Bryson to overshadow our time with Stevan. So our family, minus Bryson, traveled to Jamaica. On July 25, 2015, Stevan set foot on U.S. soil, and he was home. The complicated process, spanning one year, seven and ¼ months, had finally concluded.

Our family of six was united.

Returning home late Saturday evening, we decided to spend Sunday together, embracing the beginning of our new life as a family.

The Divine Calling that Broke Me

I was both exhausted and excited, fearful yet hopeful. I had fulfilled the Lord's calling by bringing home my fourth son. Sunday morning arrived, and after a fitful night of sleep, filled with racing thoughts, questions lingered in my mind, "What do we do now?" "How do I make him feel at home," "How do we build trust?"

Following breakfast together, Stevan expressed a desire to go outside and shoot baskets. Accompanying him, I stood outside watching him shoot baskets, and he showed me how he could balance the ball on his finger. The interaction felt awkward, and I hastily told him I was going back inside. As I walked back into the garage, I reached for the doorknob. A sudden heaviness enveloped me, and a thought echoed in my mind, "What have I done? This is going to be hard. I can't do this."

Within the first three months, it was clear the adoption wasn't going the way that I thought it would. Stevan suffered from trauma and attachment disorder. Kaden hated Stevan, Bryson remained aloof, not knowing how to comprehend the huge change in our family, and Tyrell, with his kind heart, tried to smooth things out and help. Our family remained physically together yet emotionally torn apart.

The adoption and the weight of the unknown took me to the end of myself, plunging me into the deepest depths I had ever experienced. In one of my journal entries, I wrote:

You know I am confused, overwhelmed and to be brutally honest angry. What exactly am I angry about? That is a good question. I made a statement yesterday to a friend, that "Stevan is messing up my life." I don't really know where that came from, but it came out. God I know that Brad and I answered your call, but it really sucks right now. I feel like I'm in a press and being squeezed from all sides. I have lost my joy, my desire for anything is gone.... WHY God have you taken my joy? Ok I know that you don't take my joy, but I can't figure out why it is gone. I am just going through the motions. God, I need your help, I need you but in a crazy way.... I don't want you. I am thankful that I know you are always there and, in that assurance,... I believe but it is in this performance or doing that overwhelms… ok so that doesn't come from you either but I'm tired of fighting these invisible people that I feel are forcing me to perform or behave a certain way.

God, how do I release this anger and this guilt? I feel like I must make everyone happy. There are so many responsibilities on me that the only way I can survive right now is to not feel… but it is killing me, but if I would let my walls down, I think I would cry all day and get nothing done and that isn't acceptable in my world.

I really want to run away, God, I want to run to you, I want to sit in your arms and just have you hold me… but I can't let myself, that would be letting others down.

God I'm empty… I know you want to fill me…. I don't have the energy to, it is better to just be aimless in my thoughts, going through the motions….

The call shattered me! I hadn't yet discovered healing in my identity or my journey with Bryson, and now I had brought home a 13-year-old Black Jamaican boy carrying his own trauma. Just as I had taught myself to do, I kept serving, giving, working, and gradually losing sight of myself. Anger became my constant companion. Every interaction with Bryson, Stevan, my other boys, or Brad in our marriage felt tense and overwhelming. The weight of responsibilities pressed heavily on me. Doubts crept in: did I misinterpret God's calling?

"Every day holds the possibility of a miracle," was a quote adorning the wall of our master bathroom. There were many times I contemplated taking it down, wanting to drown out its hope. Many nights saw me crying, pleading with God for answers, nestled in the tub of that very bathroom during the journey to bring Stevan home. After his arrival, I questioned the miracle I thought I wanted. Little did I know that opening my heart to a fourth son would become the transformative event that plunged me into years of depression, anger, and trauma.

My therapist undoubtedly played a crucial role during this hard time. Meeting with her every two weeks provided me with a safe place to pour out my frustrations, anger, sadness, and feelings of hopelessness. Progress seemed elusive for the first few years, but over time, through her attentive listening and guidance, she helped me navigate through the emotions, gently guiding me from irrational thoughts to a clearer understanding of truth.

While our adoption story is long and complicated and deserving of its own book, it is full of redemption and grace. Time became our ally as we navigated through the days that seemed like imprisonment, relying on God's mercy and protection. Through it, I learned that God's call may shatter you, but you're never irreparably broken. The Divine Healer patiently restores, never abandoning us in the depths but continuously drawing us back to Himself by His grace.

CHAPTER 9
Normal Please

> *"To open their eyes, so they may turn from darkness to light and from the power of Satan to God. Then they will receive forgiveness for their sins and be given a place among God's people, who are set apart by faith in me"*
>
> Acts 26:18

On a warm and muggy August night, I drove the three miles to the high school with Bryson. Bryson, who was excited and chatty. It was rare to see him nervous; confidence defined his life. However, my stomach was tied in knots, filled with anxiety, nervousness, and fear. Approaching the school, I reminded him about his bag containing juice boxes in case his blood sugar dropped. His response, as always, was a casual " I know." Without leaving the car, I pulled up to the drop-off area, and he hopped out. Bryson was prepared for this new experience, heading to his first football practice for the junior high team as a manager. Unlike him, I wasn't ready for this new experience. On the way home, I prayed for his protection and safety.

Entering junior high marked a significant transition for Bryson, moving up from elementary school. As my oldest, I found myself uncertain about the inner workings of junior high life. My only reference point was my own experiences 27 years prior, and those times had been challenging for me. Thinking about Bryson's journey, I sensed my insecurities resurfacing. That night, as I returned home, a multitude of emotions stirred within me, and a pressing question surfaced in my mind: "Do I belong? Do I fit in?"

This was not our first experience involving sports and Bryson. Bryson developed a love for sports at an early age. His first experience was at the age of eight when he joined the local county Special Olympics flag football team. His favorite position was quarterback. He soon received the nickname "the speedy bullet." He would love to draw up plays for the team with the help of his brothers. He also played on a special needs soccer team in a nearby town, and we saw how he loved playing and being part of a team. When Ty began playing at the local baseball Little League, Bryson wanted to play, too. However, we quickly realized that even at an early age, Little League could be quite competitive, requiring the right coach who was willing to make the necessary adaptations to accommodate Bryson's needs. While we could have pushed for inclusion, and I felt frustrated with the system, deep down, I knew that it might not be the best environment for him.

We discovered the Challenger Little League, where Bryson found enjoyment for several years. He had the incredible opportunity to travel with his Baugo Little League team to participate in the Little League World Series Special Needs game in Williamsport. This experience was truly a cool experience for Bryson and our family. However, after a few years, Bryson became frustrated with the Challenger League. He was becoming more knowledgeable about baseball and realized that in Challenger League, everyone got a turn to bat, and there weren't the typical three outs like in "real" baseball. To him, it didn't feel like the authentic baseball experience he wanted.

In search of a better fit, we learned that the county Special Olympics also offered softball as one of their sports. Bryson quickly found his place on the county softball team. He embraced it wholeheartedly, eagerly anticipating each practice and tournament. Bryson's role on the team revolved from playing first base or pitching, and he had a genuine passion for pitching. He would tuck his glove under his right arm, pitch with his left, and swiftly transfer the glove to his left hand, ready to catch the ball as needed. We were so impressed with how he developed this skill and how he stepped up as a leader on the team.

As my other sons, Tyrell and Kaden, started with school basketball and joined a local Christian community program called Upwards, I had a powerful desire for Bryson to be part of it as well. I thought that this Christian organization would be more compassionate and understanding toward my child. I reached out to one of the coaches within the program, but they seemed unsure about their ability to make the necessary adaptations to accommodate Bryson's needs. Once again, I heard that he couldn't play, and once again I found myself frustrated. I, again, had the option to push for inclusion. However, I made the choice to step back and let it be.

My heart ached for Bryson, and it broke once again. Then, in Bryson's sixth-grade year, a pastor whose son was in Bryson's class at school took on the role of coaching one of the teams. This pastor's involvement paved the way for Bryson to finally join a team. That year, the team welcomed Bryson with open arms, and he had an absolute blast playing alongside his friends. As a mother, I witnessed what I had longed to see – my son participating in activities just like any other child.

After Bryson played the one year with the Upwards basketball program, he joined the Special Olympics basketball team, starting out within the skills program, progressing to the three on three team, and eventually joining the five on five team. Due to his physical challenges and limited use of his right arm, shooting the ball was a challenge, but he worked diligently to develop a technique that allowed him to make baskets.

So, as seventh grade approached, Bryson knew that the school had a football team, and he expressed a strong desire to be part of the football team. My mama heart wanted him to be out there to throw, run, and be a part of the team. I saw his excitement when he played on the Special Olympics team. He believed in himself; he had dreams and aspirations. But playing football wasn't a viable option. "Real" football is hard, brutal, and there isn't a place for someone with physical disabilities on the field. My heart ached to have him be included. At Bryson's transitional IEP to junior high, the football coach, Mr. Jones, was present to discuss options. After a discussion about Bryson's challenges, Mr. Jones commented, "Bryson deserves the right to be a part of our team as much as any other kid in our school," and offered the position of football manager to Bryson. My mama heart was thrilled, and Bryson happily accepted that role.

That night after I dropped him off and was feeling all the feelings, I realized as a mother, my heart longed for him to find his place, to fit in. As I pondered the question, *"Do I belong? Do I fit in?"* I realized that was my childhood question rising inside me. I wrestled with what I wanted for my boy. I wanted his road to be different from mine. I wanted him to be involved in all the activities. I wanted his road to not be hard. My head knew that God made Bryson in His image. He created him for a purpose. But I couldn't see what that purpose was. I was blinded by my own insecurities, what the world saw as good and acceptable. I wanted to trust God that He will make a way for Bryson to fulfill the purposes that He was placed on this earth for, and that I shouldn't hinder God's work. But my heart ached with sadness!

Bryson served as manager of the football team for six years, an experience that brought him immense joy. Mr. Jones, the junior high football coach, told me later, "Bryson showed up each and every day and did whatever was asked of him. As the time went on, we had to tell him less. Eventually, he didn't need to be told; he just took over and did what needed to be done. Along the way, Bryson was not shy about sharing what he felt we should do or what play we should run.

Normal Please

He knew the game." All the football coaches and players embraced Bryson as an integral part of the team. The team's other managers collaborated exceptionally well with him, identifying his strengths and aiding him in his duties. Bryson was entrusted with the important task of delivering water to the referees during timeouts, a responsibility he executed with pride. During senior night, Bryson had the honor of carrying the flag and leading the players and coaches onto the field. It was an exhilarating moment for him!

Additionally, during his junior and senior years, he had the opportunity to manage the basketball team. Just as in football, Bryson was one of the guys. A heartwarming moment arose when the entire basketball team and coaches attended a Special Olympic basketball game to watch him play. This gesture deeply touched me and blessed my mama heart.

This sense of belonging provided him with purpose and fueled his dreams. Unlike my own insecurities and perspective on fitting in, Bryson never struggled with the question of whether he belonged.

When I discovered the book "Weird" by Craig Groeschel, with the tagline "because normal isn't working." I knew I needed to read it. Craig stated how the prevailing notion in society urges us to conform and seek approval, yet God's call is for us to be "set apart" for Him. Craig notes, "I was far more concerned with what the people thought than with what God thought." This struck a chord with me. I didn't want it to be me, but it was me! Another convicting quote echoed, "If you've surrendered to normal living rather than the wonderful weirdness of being set apart by God, chances are that people are too big in your life and God is too small"[17] In these moments of conviction, I turned to Google and searched for references to the words "set apart." My heart needed affirmation that God embraced the "weird" and "different," and I sought assurance that my son would be alright.

> "I knew you before I formed you in your mother's womb. Before you were born, I set you apart and appointed you as my prophet to the nations." Jeremiah 1:5

The struggle lies in finding the delicate balance between integrating your child into "normal" spaces while ensuring they receive the necessary support to thrive. Bryson lived in the gray area of his abilities, functioning at a higher level within the realm of "special needs" yet falling significantly below the standards of the "normal" world.

In all the different sports that Bryson participated in, most of them were "set apart" for those with disabilities. While I was glad to see him happy and engaged in these activities, I struggled with an inner turmoil. At the time I was unable to pinpoint the source of my angst. I found it difficult to attend his events. I was grateful for the opportunities he had, but it wasn't where I envisioned us being. It didn't align with the expectations I had wanted for my son. Everywhere I looked, I realized that our life wasn't following the typical path. We had to seek alternatives for everything Bryson wanted to participate in.

I didn't want to be set apart. My insecurities, my struggles with self-worth, and my difficulty in accepting Bryson's disabilities heavily influenced my perception of both him and the world around us. These feelings were deeply rooted in my past experiences, particularly during my childhood and teenage years, when I yearned to be accepted and valued for who I was. Having battled being overweight throughout my life, I had developed a habit of entering a room and instinctively scanning to see if I was the heaviest person present. Also, growing up conservative, I was required to wear dresses, skirts, and culottes always. My hair was long and uncut. I wore it in pony and piggy tails. I hated that I stood out and was different. Yet, there was my son, unmistakably different from those around him, and my heart ached because of it.

Each time Bryson participated in activities created for people with disabilities, the memories of activities that I had to participate in with my aunt Joanna surfaced. As an insecure teen myself and wrestling to find my place, the world of disabilities was a hard and scary place to be. Everywhere I looked, people were different.

Beneath the surface, I was a mother who struggled with heartbreak and questioned her faith. "*God why, why Bryson, why me?*" I was grappling with grief, denial, and the stark reality that my son, just like my Aunt Joanna, belonged in the world of disabilities and handicaps, a truth I didn't want to accept. Each new year and stage brought forth a wave of fear and uncertainty.

For years, I navigated through these hard situations, silently accumulating layers of unacknowledged grief.

The frequently heard phrase from expecting parents, "I don't care if it's a boy or a girl, as long as they are healthy," always struck a chord deep within me. While I likely uttered those same words, I didn't get the "healthy" or the "normal." My internal thoughts sometimes wanted to blurt out, "What if they aren't healthy, would you give them away?" This journey wasn't a choice I made; God chose it for me. I longed for normalcy, for the ease of a healthy child. I wanted Bryson to have all the typical experiences my other children enjoyed. Years ago, Brad shared a perspective that stuck with me, "God does not want us to be normal, He wants us different! Bryson has taught us what it means to be a child of the King. What is normal and sought after by the world is not what makes God excited. He is excited about a simple faith in him! Bryson is valuable to Jesus, just as much as the Pastor!"

Bryson wholeheartedly embraces a simple faith in Jesus, finding his foundation in the profound truth, "Jesus loves me." Unaffected by societal values, he carries an understanding that he is enough just as he is. My sweet Bryson lives unburdened by the opinions of others, his heart brimming with love for Jesus! Witnessing Bryson's unencumbered faith, I desired to inhabit the same space, free from the weight of others' opinions and swayed by the world's standards. I longed to boldly declare my belief in God's incredible plan for Bryson, seeing him through the compassionate eyes of Jesus. While my mind acknowledged the truth of this desire, my heart, at this stage of the journey, couldn't claim these truths.

CHAPTER 10

It Takes a Village

"Do all the good you can. By all the means you can. In all the ways you can. In all the places you can. At all the times you can. To all the people you can. As long as you can."
John Wesley[18]

The saying "It takes a village," often attributed to an African proverb, holds a timeless truth about the importance of community and shared responsibility. In my life, I needed a village to guide me through the challenges of raising a child with special needs. I also craved to be a part of the normal family experience. Balancing these desires became a journey of fitting into both worlds. From my childhood and throughout my life, one constant desire echoed within me – the ultimate need to fit in. This longing for acceptance and belonging has been a driving force, shaping my story and influencing my choices.

Childhood friends are priceless. They know all about you, in all the different ages of life, and they have seen you at your best and at your worst. Fran, Lynette, and I all grew up together. We went to three different high schools, and our kids were born within 20 days of each other. We could never have planned that, but God knew, God knew that I would need these lifelong friends. These friendships offered me a safe place to just be me. The safe place that Fran and Lynette offered to me extended to their daughters and the relationships formed with Bryson. God knew that Bryson would need Miranda and Lynette's daughter Ali to be his friends and support. For their 16th birthday, we went to a local photographer and took pictures of the six of us and then of the three kids. I still occasionally look at those pictures and thank God for how he orchestrated our friendships and that of our kids!

> "Long friendships are like jewels, polished over time to become beautiful and enduring." Celia Brayfield[19]

Playdates were a bright spot in my life, offering a break from the routine of weekly therapies, appointments, and the everyday challenges of being a mom. Amidst the busyness, these gatherings represented a slice of normalcy, something all normal moms seem to do. Over the years, a group of four to six moms regularly gathered, bringing their children together for moments of fun and connection. Whether meeting at homes, children's museums, parks, or holiday gatherings, the kids outnumbered the moms, forming friendships while we enjoyed moments of laughter, conversation, and shared advice. In these playdates, I found a space where I wasn't a special needs mom; I was simply "mom." It wasn't always easy, but Tyrell and Kaden seamlessly blended in, and the children accepted Bryson just as he was.

> "Alone we can do so little. Together we can do so much."
> Hellen Keller[20]

My mother, Wilma, affectionately known as Mamma by her grandchildren and many children in my village, radiates love to all who cross her path. Despite walking a challenging road, marked by the loss of her husband and my father when she was 56, her heart remained open and vulnerable. His passing took a toll, especially as she continued to care for her sister Joanna.

When I shared the news that I was expecting my first child, Bryson, my mother was extremely excited but her joy for me was clouded with the sadness that my children would never know their gentle and soft-spoken grandfather. When news of Bryson's challenges unfolded after his birth, my mom became my biggest supporter. Throughout her life, she had selflessly given for the well-being of others, and despite her own hardships, she ensured that Bryson felt special from the very beginning.

My mother dove headfirst into Bryson's world, offering her unwavering support with therapies, doctor's appointments, household tasks, and meals. Over the years, she took Bryson to therapy, picked him up from preschool, took him to Special Olympic practices, and later football and basketball practice. She even dropped him off and picked him up from his job after high school. Learning to administer his seizure medication and later managing his diabetes care, she embraced every aspect of Bryson's care.

As Bryson's world transitioned after high school, Mamma stepped in to provide him with new opportunities. Their bond was extraordinary, with special times carved out for Bryson every Monday night at her house. Spoiled might be an understatement, as they indulged in their tradition of visiting Fazoli's for breadsticks on Saturday evenings.

My mom was my rock, offering the respite I needed. She understood the challenges of navigating the world of disabilities and stood by me, providing a safe space for Bryson and me. While her tears often fell, I had learned to suppress my tears. Often, I felt the need to escape when her eyes teared up. I wanted to release my tears, but I didn't know how. I read that a grandparent's grief is two-fold. They grieve not just for their child but also for their grandchild. In her tears, I discovered both the depth of her love and the shared sorrow for the challenges that Bryson faced. Witnessing my mother's sorrow only deepened my own sense of grief.

Another trip to the orthopedic office, and as the saying goes, if it isn't one thing, it's another. This time, Bryson had dislocated his kneecap and cracked off the corner during Special Olympics basketball practice. Arriving for a follow-up appointment, Bryson, donning his knee brace, followed me into the cramped temporary office. The waiting area was compact, with chairs lined up on each side and a small section of four chairs facing the door sitting in the middle. As I entered, I noticed my friend Dawn straight ahead. We had known each other over the years, both navigating the challenges of raising sons with multiple disabilities. It had been a while since our last encounter, and we took the chance to catch up on our families and the reasons for the current visit to the orthopedic office. Interestingly, Dawn wasn't there for her special son but for another son who had sustained an injury at a sporting event. We shared a chuckle over the perpetual extra challenges we faced.

Amidst our conversation, Dawn casually mentioned, "Last month, my friend Becky started a special needs moms' group. We have just met once. Would you be interested in coming next month?" In that fleeting moment, I found exactly what I had been searching for- a place where I could be known and understood. I had previously spoken to other moms, but plans never materialized for meetings. This prospect of joining this special needs moms' group filled me with excitement and anticipation, a welcomed opportunity to connect with kindred spirits who shared similar journeys.

And so began my involvement in Moms Need Moms – a vibrant, resilient, feisty, and fantastic group of ladies bounded together by the shared title of "special needs mom." Our monthly gatherings became a sanctuary where heart-wrenching stories were shared, and the simplest steps of the process were celebrated with the same fanfare as a graduation ceremony. Laughter, common in our meetings, often sparked by comments about our children and the unconventional strategies we employed. We'd jokingly say, "If a normal person heard this, they would probably turn us into CPS." Our actions weren't born out of a desire to harm but rather of necessity as we creatively navigated the unique challenges we faced.

One year, we decided to commemorate our shared journey with shirts bearing the message, "As a mother, my job is to take care of the possible and trust God with the impossible,"[21] a quote by Ruth Bell Graham. God brought me to this incredible group when Bryson was 13, wishing I had found this support network in those early years. Nonetheless, I embraced the opportunity to both receive encouragement and share my experiences.

Finding this group of moms was like discovering a balm for my weary soul. For so long, I had struggled with the desire to "fit in." But this group, surrounded by compassionate women, I found my safe place. Here, our words were the "normal" ones, understood and empathized by all. We shared a unique bond born out of our shared experiences, allowing us to truly connect and support one another in a way that only those who have walked the path of disability could understand.

As I pen this chapter, our group continues to meet regularly. These ladies, often exhausted and overwhelmed, face an uncertain future for their special children. Yet, they stand as warriors, selflessly giving of themselves every day for their children and families. They cling to God for the hope and peace that only He can provide. I love each of them dearly and am immensely proud to call them friends!

> **Friendship is born at the moment when one person says to another: 'What! You too? I thought I was the only one.'" C.S. Lewis**[22]

Bryson, like me, needed a village to – a community that provided him with constant support, love, and attention. Gratefully, through my close friendships, he found his own village, a dependable network that surrounded him with care and understanding.

In the beauty of God's plan, the lives of Fran's daughter, Miranda, and Bryson began four days apart. Their initial encounter, when Bryson was a mere six days old and Miranda only two, set the stage for a remarkable friendship that would blossom over the years.

As we introduced them that first time, promising a world of shared adventures and joyful moments, little did we know how profoundly their lives would intertwine. From that moment, Bryson and Miranda formed a bond that resembled the closeness of siblings. Their connection was sweet and real, easily overshadowing any differences that might have existed.

In their early years, their togetherness was more a product of Fran's and my friendship. Yet, as the seasons changed, so did the nature of their friendship. Their shared love of sports was at the forefront of most of their activities. Countless games of football, basketball, and hockey were played from our unfinished basement, affectionately named the "hockey room," or our front yard. I often heard shouts of "go long" and touchdown" and bursts of laughter echoing through the house. The unmistakable blare of Veggie Tales and the Wiggles soundtracks coming from Miranda's car each time she arrived to pick up Bryson for another adventure. The laughter that ensued during these car rides was legendary, with tales later shared of intense laughter resulting in tears.

A shared passion for the Chicago Cubs and the Indianapolis Colts led to many memorable trips to Wrigley Field and Lucas Oil Stadium. The electric fever of the 2016 Cubs World Series run created an unforgettable experience for Bryson and Miranda, watching games together, cheering and screaming for every heart-pounding game.

The profound uniqueness in their relationship touches the depth of my soul. Fran, with her kind and loving spirit, embraced the friendship between our children, never drawing attention to the differences for Miranda. It wasn't until their teenage years that Miranda became more aware of Bryson's disabilities. Yet, to Miranda, she didn't see his disabilities. Bryson remained Bryson. Her compassionate heart allowed her to see beyond limitations and focus on the passion that fueled Bryson's spirit.

A poignant chapter in their friendship unfolded when Bryson stood proudly as a groomsman at Miranda's wedding. This quarter-century friendship has not just given life to Bryson; it has also shaped him into the confident young man he is today. The enduring beauty of their friendship transcends time, a testament to the power of unconditional love.

Ali, born two weeks before Bryson, mirrored Miranda's compassionate heart. Despite not spending time together at social events, they found their connection through the children's department at church. Ali's mom, Lyn, served as children's director, and I often found myself serving with Lyn. Ali and Bryson's relationship also resembled the closeness of siblings.

Ali's parents, Gordon and Lyn, went above and beyond to shower Bryson with the love and attention he craved. Gordon, a pilot, took Bryson for an airplane ride one Saturday afternoon ride when Bryson was two years old. Their family wholeheartedly embraced Bryson as one of their own, fostering a sense of belonging that exceeded mere friendship. Together they offered a support network that provided Bryson with the understanding and care he needed.

However, life took an unexpected turn when Ali's family relocated to the Phoenix area during Bryson's junior year of high school. This separation marked a challenging period for Bryson, as the weekly conversations and hangout sessions ended. Despite the physical distance, the bonds forged during their time together remained strong.

Interestingly, this chapter in Bryson's life planted a seed in his mind – a dream of someday moving to Arizona. The closeness and acceptance he experienced with their family became a beacon of hope, inspiring him to dream of a new chapter in the warm and sunny landscape of the Southwest.

The chime of my phone heralded a surprising text message from Ali: "Bryson just called me and asked me to go to his senior prom with him. Thoughts?" Initially taken aback, a surge of pride followed as I realized the bravery it took for Bryson to reach out on his own. Although he had expressed his desire to attend prom, my typical response had been to avoid the topic, hoping it would simply fade away. This parenting approach, rooted in my insecurities, wasn't good, but the prospect seemed daunting. I wanted him to attend, but fear overshadowed.

After a few moments of contemplation, I responded to Ali, "Let me think about it. Are you willing to do this with Bryson?" Her reply was swift, "I'm willing if we can figure out the details." Despite living 1900 miles away in Arizona, Ali and Bryson's relationship remained close.

Over the next several months, numerous text messages and phone calls exchanged as we planned every detail. On a cloudy April Thursday afternoon, Bryson, Miranda, and I drove to the South Bend airport to welcome Ali. It was a beautiful reunion of three friends, with Ali's return to Indiana proving to be emotional.

The Saturday of prom was a whirlwind of activity as I assisted Bryson in donning his black tuxedo, accompanied by a pale mauve tie and vest. Nervous yet excited, he waited as a bright yellow Mini Cooper, borrowed from Ali's uncle, pulled into the driveway. Stepping out of the car in a soft mauve floor-length dress, Ali's beautiful, curled blond hair flowed in the wind. The afternoon spring breeze was cold, especially for Ali, who strongly dislikes cold weather. But the warmth of friendship enveloped us as we headed into the backyard for pictures. With some assistance, Bryson placed a wrist corsage on Ali to match his boutonniere, and his smile never wavered.

As they drove out of the driveway to the school, my heart swelled with gratitude for Ali's extraordinary kindness and friendship. She didn't attend the same high school as Bryson, entering a prom where she knew no one else, yet she did so because she recognized the significance of this moment for Bryson.

Bryson, proudly escorting Ali, enjoyed this rite of passage as a senior in high school. The pictures of Bryson dancing and mingling with Ali and other friends were precious to me. Ali had gone the extra mile, or rather 1900 miles, to provide Bryson with the opportunity to cherish this special moment.

> **Be strong, be fearless, be beautiful. And believe that anything is possible when you have the right people there to support you." Misty Copeland**[23]

The village that embraced Bryson and me extended far beyond, encompassing extended family and cherished friends who stood by us through the challenges of this journey. The immense blessing of Brad's large family was evident as I found myself surrounded and embraced in their unwavering support and love. Bryson, in turn, experienced many fun-filled and exciting adventures with his uncles, aunts and cousins.

I came to the realization, surrounded by family, close friends and my Moms Need Moms group, that they truly knew me and loved me, the need to "fit in" evaporated, replaced by a sense of belonging and unspoken understanding. It is within this amazing circle of support that I discovered the strength to continue to march forward, championing the best for Bryson.

CHAPTER 11

Identity

> *"All our promises and resolutions end in denial because we don't have the power to accomplish them. We must come to the end of ourselves and receive the Holy Spirit and His power will invade us and accomplish much."*
> Oswald Chambers[24]

Under the warm embrace of a sunny Sunday afternoon, the front yard of our home became a bustling arena of activity. The air was alive with contagious energy. My boys and several of the neighbor boys and dads immersed themselves in a rowdy game of football. Meanwhile, I was in my office catching up on some tasks.

The cheers and laughter were only a faint whisper where I sat, but suddenly, a piercing scream echoed through the air. An immediate surge of concern flooded my thoughts as I abandoned my work and headed for the door. The garage door swung open, revealing Bryson, his face contorted with a mix of anger and tears. Following closely behind was Brad, ushering Bryson into the house and to his bedroom.

Brad explained that Bryson was mad because his team had lost the game.

When Bryson struggled to understand a situation, he would become frustrated, leading to screaming, crying, and occasionally violence. Brad and I stood in the hallway, deliberating on the best approach to address Bryson's emotional outburst. Brad ventured into the room, engaging Bryson in a conversation. "Bryson, in sports, there is always a team that loses. Remember when Peyton Manning lost the Super Bowl? Did he start screaming and get mad?". Brad continued, "Good sportsmanship is how we handle ourselves when we lose. No one likes to lose." Bryson, with his tear-streaked face, looked up at Brad, "But dad, I don't want to be a loser," he said as he lifted his left hand and made an L sign on his forehead. "I want to be a winner." Brad, suppressing a laugh, reassured him "Bryson, just because you lose at a game doesn't make you a loser."

The tension dissipated as Bryson, now calmer, rejoined the boys outside, continuing to toss the football in the front yard. However, for me, the incident lingered, tugging at the strings of my mother's heart. Questions surfaced- did Bryson perceive himself as different, as a loser in life? The instinct to shield him from such perceptions overwhelmed me. Sadly, I saw myself in his questions.

The desire to be winners by the world's standards is often based on education, performance, finances, and appearance. Memories of my childhood surfaced, confirming my ongoing struggle with feeling like a loser in those areas. As I sat down at my desk again, I sought refuge in the words of Psalms 139: 13-16, "You made all the delicate, inner parts of my body and knit me together in my mother's womb. Thank you for making me so wonderfully complex! Your workmanship is marvelous—how well I know it. You watched me as I was being formed in utter seclusion, as I was woven together in the dark of the womb. You saw me before I was born. Every day of my life was recorded in your book. Every moment was laid out before a single day had passed." In that vulnerable moment, I found peace in the divine craftsmanship spoken in the sacred verse; these words a grounding reassurance.

Bryson and I were fearfully and wonderfully made.

"Exciting news, team!" Coach Mary Lou exclaimed as her little league players gathered around her after the game. "Our team has been invited to represent Indiana in the Challenger game during the Little League World Series." Bryson and his teammates erupted in cheers at the announcement. The opportunity to go to Williamsport was a once-in-a-lifetime event. Each year, only two teams were selected from the Challenger League to participate in the special game, providing children with disabilities the chance to showcase their talents on the grand stage. Our family, thrilled to support Bryson in this incredible event, eagerly set out for Pennsylvania.

The air was thick with anticipation as the Indiana Challenger Baseball team prepared to engage in a game against their counterparts from Louisiana at the prestigious Little League World Series in Williamsport, Pennsylvania. The night before the game, both teams were invited to a welcome party generously hosted by local businesses.

As the members and families of Bryson's team settled beneath the expansive white tent, the aroma of shared excitement mingled with the tantalizing scent of food. Seated beside Bryson, I couldn't help feeling a sense of pride in the unique journey his team was undertaking. Before long, the atmosphere shifted with the arrival of the opposing team from Louisiana. Bryson's attention, keenly observant, fixated on the approaching players. A moment of quick reflection followed, and then, with genuine curiosity, he turned to me, his innocent eyes searching for understanding. "Mom, the other team is handicapped!" he exclaimed, his words hanging in the air. My challenge lay in crafting a response that acknowledged the truth while navigating the emotions intertwined with Bryson's statement. With a tender smile, I replied, "Yes, they are." However, as I answered, an internal dialogue unfolded. Did Bryson grasp the realization that he, too, was handicapped? Did he recognize the distinctiveness of the team he belonged to, a team that defied the conventional norms of "normal" Little League teams?

In the quiet moments of reflection over the weekend, the resonance of Bryson's innocent observation lingered in my thoughts. As I unpacked the layers of our short conversation, a realization unfolded – Bryson's perception of himself was not confined in the realm of his handicaps but rather in the vast landscape of opportunities that he had been given.

Bryson has consistently approached life focusing on what he CAN do, undeterred by any discouragement stemming from what he CANNOT do. Reflecting on my life, I pondered the lens through which I perceived life. What were the pivotal factors shaping my outlook on life?

As a mother of a special needs kid, I see special needs kids everywhere, and I see their mothers everywhere.

As a mother of boys, I see boys and their mothers everywhere as they interact, discipline, and love each other.

When I hear that someone has lost their father, I mourn with them because I have lost mine.

When I see or hear another woman struggling with low self-esteem, fear, weight issues, and pride. I can relate because I've been there.

Upon reflecting on my thoughts, I set out to challenge myself. Was I solely focusing on the negative aspects and the hardships that I was enduring? Realizing that the handicaps in my own life could serve as a catalyst for helping others in dealing with, coping, and overcoming their own handicaps was a transformative revelation. At the tender age of 13, Bryson had already grasped the profound concept of viewing life through God's lens. I, too, needed to view life through God's lens.

I could be a conduit of His love, a vessel to offer life and hope to those around me.

Bryson's anticipation of his birthdays was palpable, with months of chatter preceding the day. He meticulously detailed his wish for gifts, party themes, and the select few he wanted to invite to the party. While I honored his requests for themes and gifts, I cautiously skirted around the guest list, restricting it to family and a handful of close family friends, but never his peers.

The buzz of birthday preparations began shortly after the Christmas holidays, culminating in Bryson's late January celebration. His desire for a Peyton Manning Fathead took center stage, accompanied by an enthusiastic recitation of boys' names he hoped to invite, including Reuben, Sethen and Mitchell. Reuben and Bryson shared a special education para, Mrs. Johnson, and developed a unique bond. Sethen and Mitchell were friends through school and church.

Struggling with the decision of whether to host a larger party with more friends, I eventually opted for another small gathering. Finally, birthday week arrived. His birthday fell on Thursday, the night of his Special Olympics basketball practice. I revealed my plan to Bryson for a post-practice Pizza Hut celebration with Reuben and Tyler, a Special Olympics teammate. Disappointment etched across Bryson's face, yet he maintained a stoic silence, choosing not to verbalize his feelings.

However, complications arose on Wednesday night when Mitchell's mom, Lisa, approached me at church with an inquiry, "Lisa, I have a weird question for you. Is there a birthday party for Bryson on Thursday night?" I froze. Bryson must have invited Mitchell to his party. "Mitchell really likes Bryson and is excited about the party," Lisa continued. I felt an angst in my spirit. "We are just having several boys come to Pizza Hut for supper, not planning on too many people," I explained. "I will explain this to Mitchell," Lisa responded. A surge of emotions stirred within me; the question echoed in my mind: *Do these boys genuinely like my son?* In that moment of introspection, my true motive revealed itself – I was playing it safe. The colors of my true intentions emerged, exposing the fact that I was selectively inviting only those boys whom I was certain liked my son. Despite knowing that Bryson had friends at school, I was not giving them a chance to be a part of his celebration. I felt a tinge of guilt, but I just wanted this situation to go away.

The next morning brought a phone call from Sethen's mom, Kathleen. "Lisa, what time exactly and where is Bryson's birthday party tonight?" I couldn't speak. She went on, "Bryson called me two weeks ago and told me about having a party and invited Sethen and it was going to be a Peyton Manning party and I was to buy him a gift." My heart sank. "Kathleen, I'm so sorry that he called you." "No need to apologize, I thought it was sweet." Kathleen responded, "Sethen has been talking about it for the past few weeks and is super excited to come." My heart convicted, I said, "Kathleen let's do this, I will pick up Sethen at 6 pm, and we will surprise Bryson at Pizza Hut." I immediately called Lisa, Mitchell's mom, and told her the new plan.

I called Brad after my phone conversation with Kathleen, telling him what had transpired. In his profound wisdom, he said, "If asked the question. 'Why did God allow people to be born with disabilities?' God allowed people to be born on this earth with disabilities to test those of us who encounter them as to what our hearts really are like."

I forced myself to confront my reservations and reevaluate my motives. Was I protecting Bryson or shielding myself from potential discomfort? As the hard truth washed over me in shame, I realized I had been playing God in Bryson's life, concealing him from potential friendships. I didn't want to be different as a child, and I didn't want my child to be different, either. But mine was different. Despite convincing myself that I had accepted this reality, a harsh truth struck me- Had I truly embraced it?

I heard often what a great friend Bryson was to everyone. The tug of truth compelled me to reevaluate and consider the impact of my actions on Bryson's life and the missed opportunities for others to love, care for, and befriend Bryson. This difficult moment of introspection challenged me to open my heart wider. I once again was viewing Bryson through my own tinted glasses rather than seeing him how God does. I realized I needed to trust that others also have Bryson's best interests at heart, just as God does, and allow them to love my son.

The birthday party was a time of fun and laughter at Pizza Hut. Bryson's friend, Ben, another Special Olympics teammate, and his mom, Monica, joined the celebration. Bryson was so excited when he saw Sethen and Mitchell. (they hid under the table when he came in) The love and friendship among the boys, proving that differences held no significance, was beautiful to watch. Bryson, once again, became my teacher, emphasizing the need to broaden my social circles, open my heart to others, and allow the goodness of friendship and God's love to fill my life.

Learning from the truth of my actions, the next year, on Bryson's 13th birthday, I took deliberate steps to rectify my past failures. I reserved the gym at the local Christian school, extending invitations to all his classmates, teachers, church friends, Special Olympics teammates, family, and anyone who knew him. The result was an extravagant party. The air was filled with his favorite worship music, the gym resonated with the thud of basketballs in a spirited tournament, and I made sure to serve all his favorite foods.

Over 100 people, a mix of classmates, teachers, friends, and family, gathered to shower Bryson with love and appreciation, demonstrating just how valued he was. Bryson embraced the joy of the occasion, unaware of the depth of my reflection from the previous year. That night became a pivotal moment, a redemptive act born out of the mistakes I had made in the past. Grateful for the opportunity to amend what I had previously withheld, the celebration marked a renewed commitment to ensuring Bryson felt accepted for the incredible person he is.

"Our deepest fear is not that we are inadequate. Our deepest fear is that we are powerful beyond measure. It is our light, not our darkness, that most frightens us. We ask ourselves, "Who am I to be brilliant, gorgeous, talented and fabulous?" Actually, who are you not to be? You are a child of God. Our playing small doesn't serve the world. There's nothing enlightened about shrinking so that other people won't feel insecure around you. We were born to manifest the glory of God that is within us…And as we let our own light shine, we unconsciously give other people permission to do the same. As we are liberated from our own fear, our presence automatically liberates others."
Marianne Williamson[25]

CHAPTER 12

On Board the Grief Train

"The dance of life finds its beginnings in grief. It is the way in which pain can be embraced, not out of a desire to suffer, but in the knowledge that something new will be born in our pain."
Henri Nouwen[26]

Tuesdays were the day that I had a babysitter for Bryson, and I went to work. It was an outlet for me, a space where I could be something other than a mother and all the added responsibilities that had become a part of my daily life with Bryson. Bryson was two years old and, on this particular Tuesday, I was in a difficult place. I felt my confusion and anger swirling inside me. I had found a way to hold these emotions tight within. I wanted Bryson HEALED! I wanted to know the WHY from God. *"God why, after all I had done to help care for Joanna, why, God, I told you I didn't want a handicapped child."* I knew that day I wasn't going to be able to concentrate on my work, so I decided to head for the local mall in search of a resource, a book, something to help me in this hard situation I was in.

As I walked in from the parking lot, I prayed that I would find exactly what I needed. It was a short, dark, lit hall that I entered. It wasn't the main entrance of the mall; this one was the shortest way to the Christian bookstore. The store was bright, and off to the left were all the bright-colored gift ideas. The left side harbored the DVD racks; I loved looking through those. Music was often a balm to my soul, and we had discovered how much music calmed Bryson's cries many times.

I headed straight to the rows of books, each section nicely labeled with what the books were about. I had searched for books on special needs children before, but I had struggled to find many. The inventory appeared slim. I went to the family aisle and poured through the contents. There on the bottom shelf a bright blue book with rainbow words, "Extraordinary KIDS" shouted out to me. I picked it up. The tagline was "nurturing and championing your child with special needs." I leafed through the pages and felt this glimmer of hope. This book was going to provide for me what I was longing for… hope and answers to my many questions.

After browsing through the remainder of the store, I purchased the book and went to work. My spirits felt lighter. I had a resource. I would find the answers for which I was longing. After Bryson was in bed that evening, I sat down in the corner recliner chair in the living room, curled up with a soft, cozy blanket, and I settled in to read. As I read, I became restless, and I felt my body tighten. The words offended me. I felt appalled at what I was reading. They made it seem easy and implied that it will all work out. I made myself skim through the chapters, but I couldn't finish it. This book didn't help; it made me feel worse. That night, I went to bed more discouraged and hopeless. *Would I ever find what I needed?*

During this period of searching, I joined a prayer group of ladies from church. It was an intimate gathering. As we gathered in different women's homes, there was a feeling of safety and vulnerability that was present. Each time we met, I opened my heart and soul to these wonderful women, sharing my fears, anger, and my longing for my son's healing. Each time I shared, they surrounded me with love and prayed that I would understand and receive God's love for both me and my child. As we prayed, I would fervently cry out for my son's healing.

It was several weeks after I had skimmed through the book about children with special needs, and I knew that I needed these ladies to pray for me and to surround me. The evening, as usual, started with singing worship songs, and I felt myself receiving the peace that my soul needed at that moment. As I was ushered into the presence of the Holy Spirit, I knew I had come to a safe place to share. I poured out my heart to them. I told them how I had purchased this book about "extraordinary kids" and how it had offended and appalled me. As I released my angry emotions to them, with tears flowing, "I don't understand. I want to have something that will help me." The ladies came around me and laid their hands on me and prayed. As we finished praying, one lady quietly spoke, "Lisa, just throw it away and forget it. This book wasn't what you needed." I thanked her, and as I went home that night, I picked up the book and headed for the trash can. Thoughts entered my mind that I should just burn it. But as I was ready to toss it, I couldn't do it. I don't know if it was because I love books and couldn't throw the book away. Instead, I carried it into my bedroom and buried it in the back corner of my closet.

Nine months later, while cleaning out boxes in my closet, I stumbled upon the book that I had hidden. As I picked up the book, I felt an urge to read it. I didn't understand, I recalled the emotions that I had the first time. But I knew I had to read it again. I had to give the book another chance.

Again, it was evening, and I sat on my recliner in the corner of the living room, wrapped in my cozy blanket, and I started reading. I couldn't put the book down. I read, I cried, I read more, and I cried. My heart and my mind soaked in each word on the pages. I felt God's presence breathing on me, and I sat and read the entire book. As I finished, I knew that I had just read a powerful book and that God had orchestrated this encounter for this time.

As I pondered the changes that had taken place in the past nine months, I questioned why the impact of the book felt different now than it did the first time I read it. It became clear that God had been at work within me, softening my heart, revealing truth, and guiding me toward accepting the reality of being a mother to a special needs child. I had reached a point where I was open and ready to embrace the truth!

This acceptance marked a shift in my perspective, reducing the urgency to cry out for Bryson's healing. Instead, it led me to a new stage where I started examining the motives behind my desire for his healing. Did I seek healing solely for Bryson's benefit, or was it influenced by my own convenience? Was I trying to avoid the daily routine of administering seizure medication, the time-consuming therapies, or the judgments of others?

In my vulnerability, I realized that remnants of my childhood struggles still lingered. I had acknowledged my role as a special needs mom, but my heart was not ready to embrace the complete journey of grief.

> **The way in which a man accepts his fate and all the suffering it entails, the way in which he takes up his cross, gives him ample opportunity – even under the most difficult circumstances – to add a deeper meaning to his life.**
> **Victor Frankl**[27]

As the clock approached midnight, another sleepless night loomed before me. The week had been emotionally taxing- it was the week of the local county fair. The fair was always a highlight for our family. However, this year, the fair had served as a stark reminder of my son's placement in the disability world, triggering a torrent of grief within me. While I had faced similar reminders before, this night, the heaviness that engulfed me as I lay in bed was suffocating.

Unable to bear the weight of my emotions any longer, I forced myself out of bed and made my way to the computer. I knew that writing was my lifeline, a means of releasing the pent-up thoughts and feelings swirling inside me. As I sat before the screen, my legs trembled with tension, my stomach churned with nausea, and my fingers flew across the keyboard, desperately trying to keep pace with the torrent of thoughts flooding my mind.

With each keystroke, I poured out every event, every moment, every painful memory that had plagued me, starting with the most recent from the week. The words flowed from me like a rushing river, carrying with them a mixture of sadness, anger, and a wall of grief. Writing became my sanctuary, my therapy and as I continued to pour my heart out onto the screen, tears began to blur my vision and fall onto the keyboard. But at that moment, I didn't care. Each keystroke felt like a cathartic release, a way of sharing my pain with someone, anyone who would listen. With each word, I felt a weight lifting from my chest, as if the act of writing was loosening the suffocating grip of grief.

Below are the memories I wrote about that night.

Monday, I carried a bright orange paper to the fair which declared Disability Awareness Day. It was a bright orange and a bold reminder that my son qualified for that. He participated in the 5 skill events that were set up for those with disabilities, most of which were way below his level. He did them, and we cheered. He won the basketball shooting skill and made it into an article in the local newspaper about "Special Needs Day" at the fair.

All three of my boys participated Monday afternoon in the 3-point shot barn ball competition at the fair. Bryson played with the "normal" boys. He got lots of cheers!! He and Ty both sank 5 out of 10 baskets in their age group and participated in a shootout with four other boys. I cheered

against the others; Bryson missed his shot. I was super proud of him and glad that he could participate in this, but I wanted him to win. I want him to be normal.

Ty and Kaden both have gone to the fair with friends; Bryson has asked me about him going with his friends… I skirted the subject; I told him how much fun he will have with his "PAID FRIEND" (respite worker) on Thursday when he goes with him. I hated it. I had to pay someone to take Bryson to the fair. He had friends at school, but this was summer, the typical teenage experiences of hanging out at friends' houses and engaging in social activities were absent. Bryson didn't often express his feelings about this, but I saw the sadness in his eyes when he learned about what his friends were doing. He wasn't receiving invitations to the fair, birthday parties, trips to the beach, or movie nights.

At Special Olympics softball practice on Thursday night, he got to pitch, just what he always wanted to do. He pitched with accuracy and strength. As I sat on the sidelines, I studied him as he tucked his mitt under his right arm, pitched the ball, and then hurried and put his hand into his mitt. He caught the ball returned from the catcher, put the mitt under his right arm, again pulled the ball out and did it again. He did it for almost one and half hours. He was HAPPY! During his batting practice, he went through the motions of swinging his bat just like the big leaguers do. He hit the ball, but the ball just went into the outfield because the others on the team had lost interest a long time ago. As we walked out away from the field, I felt it in my spirit, Bryson got to do what he wanted. He was excited and proud of what he was doing, but he knew nobody else really cares about this like he does. No one was cheering for him. No one saw what he was capable of. I cried inside to myself, "Does anybody care?" He never complains, but that night I felt it in the silence from him... It hurts!

Mom, when can I drive?" Bryson repeatedly asks. At 16 years old, he sees his friend's pictures and posts of driver's licenses popping up on his Facebook page. Over and over, I respond, "Not at this time, Bryson." "Why won't you let me drive?" Bryson's accusing words of blame slam deep into my soul: A constant reminder of limitations.

Bryson loves football, but he is on the sidelines. He loves to be a manager, but he knows he will never play in a real game. Even with the limitations of his right arm, he has a mean, accurate, and a good throw. But who sees that? All the things that Bryson does well are performed in our front yard, barns at the fair, or ball diamonds with the Special Olympics, where no one sees because he can't be on the field. He will be on the sidelines in all things "normal" sports related.

Why God, Why TYPE 1 DIABETES, THERE IS NO CURE! This is a life sentence. This disease has caused him to be more dependent on others than his other mental and physical disabilities in lots of ways.

We all yearn for love and to be loved in return. Bryson possesses the physical tendencies as a typical male, but emotionally, mentally, and socially he faces unique challenges. I didn't have the strength to come out and say, "Bryson, you may never have a girlfriend or get married."

As I finished pouring out all my words, I told God, "I don't understand your playing rules; I know there are all sorts of Bible verses that can be quoted, and deep down, I know truth", but in the darkness of that midnight hour, I wanted to pound my fists and roar loudly in pain, but instead I climbed back into bed, wept into my pillow and prayed the pain would go away.

> **So you have sorrow now, but I will see you again; then you will rejoice, and no one can rob you of that joy. John 16:22**

Many times over the years, Brad and I fought with each other. Our fights were not screaming matches, and many times didn't involve many words. We both struggled with being passive-aggressive and sometimes that was worse than just screaming at each other. Yes, fighting is normal in marriage, but when unique circumstances and grief are involved, it takes these conflicts to a new level. No two people grieve the same way. From my reading in various books on grief, I've come to understand that every individual's experience of grief is unique. However, a universal aspect is the desire for acknowledgment. Regardless of our grieving methods, we desire to be seen. We don't want reassurances or attempts to diminish our sorrow. Instead, we long for someone to walk with us fully in our grief, without the need to find a silver lining.

The path of grief is not linear; it is up and down, forward, and backward. It has its own dance. As I struggled to deal with responsibilities and was unaware of the real underlying battle that was going on, my anger and frustrations often were taken out on Brad. He didn't understand, he didn't help enough, he didn't care enough. We were one in marriage, and we were both the parents of Bryson, but truthfully, we were two individuals searching to make sense of our son's disabilities and what the future would look like. I learned early on in my time searching for help and answers. The divorce rate for couples with special needs children is staggering: 80%. I get it. I understand why. The symptoms of grief are excruciating.

One evening, as I was upset and taking it out on Brad, "Why don't you get it? Why don't you understand how I feel? Are you even feeling anything?" I questioned. Brad strongly disliked conflict, and in this moment, his normal tendency would have been to retreat. Instead he quietly replied, "Can I tell you a story of one of my saddest moments?" I quietly sat down, ashamed of my accusations of him. Brad went on to share this with me.

"Lisa, the other Saturday when I took Bryson to Loveway, my emotions shifted from sadness to outright anger. The memory of that waiting room is still vivid in my mind. The staff at Loveway were exceptionally kind, showering Bryson with affection as they prepared him for the ride. Bryson rode a grayish-colored horse. It was just the right horse for him. The weather was pleasant, so we went outside, with Bryson making laps around the ring, guided by one person leading the horse and one on the right and left to ensure his safety.

As I settled into the portable bleaches provided for "spectators," my thoughts began to drift. Initially, I wondered if Bryson genuinely enjoyed the experience, but my mind soon wandered to work projects and if horseback riding would truly improve his life. Slowly, I became aware of my surroundings and the stark reality. I was sitting next to the small riding arena with the smell of horses, watching my son and this horse getting led in circles by THREE people. And I was sitting on these tired bleachers by myself, no less, watching all this. This is bullshit. I am sitting on these bleachers watching my son getting paraded around by these people on this horse that I wasn't sure either Bryson or I even liked. I knew my friends were also sitting on the bleachers. But they were sitting on the bleachers watching their kids play T-ball. They had lots of friends sitting near them. Their kids had friends they were interacting with. I was sure they even had popcorn! All I had was my disabled son being paraded around this ring that smelled like horse shit. The longer I sat there, the more bitter and angry I became. It's not fair. Not to me. Not to Bryson.

Brad continued, "Lisa, I see your pain. I hurt for you almost greater than I hurt for Bryson. In many ways, you have the handicaps.

You monitor his medications, take him to therapy, doctor visits, and advocate for him. My grief is twice over for you and him and, knowing it is not a sickness, but a lifelong condition. I feel sadness, lots of sadness."

As we sat together after, a renewed bond developed between us. I now had heard his heart; I heard the depth of his grief and I no longer feel alone on the journey.

> **Watching your child hurt is one of the biggest sources of grief you can feel. Grief still lingers today; it never goes away totally, but I had a choice to make.**

Grief manifests itself, often unexpectedly, sometimes daily, sometimes hourly, showing its ugly face. Its timing never seemed right. I can confidently say that I've walked through each of the five stages of grief - denial, anger, bargaining, depression, and acceptance - many times. For the initial ten months, denial became my dwelling place, and denial continued to show its hand at other times over the years.

Anger became a familiar companion, often expressed in silent frustration, sharp words, put-downs, and tears due to my perception that anger was wrong. It was only later, after I realized God was okay with my anger, that I found comfort in screaming, crying out and questioning.

The bargaining stage felt like my expertise. Control, Brad might say, was my middle name. Managing all of Bryson's needs wasn't my duty alone but a way for me to feel in control, and to feel capable of managing all the responsibilities. My desire was to find a solution or influence the situation in a way that would stop the pain and sadness. I crafted numerous "what if" and "if only" scenarios, all with the determination to make Bryson's life the best it could be

Depression, a messy and challenging stage, surfaced multiple times over the years. It profoundly affected my mood, energy level, and ability to function. It was a heavy and confusing burden which drained all hope and joy from my spirit.

Acceptance, often considered the final stage, is like the caboose on a train. In the past, the caboose marked the end of the train. But today, the caboose is rarely seen. However, when spotted, it's usually somewhere in the middle of the train, suggesting acceptance isn't the end. Acceptance is indeed a challenging process that requires significant effort and introspection. Barriers such as fear of the unknown, loss of control, emotional turmoil, resistance to change, and the struggle to let go of expectations can all impede the journey toward acceptance. I had to wrestle through many of those barriers in various situations and experiences along the way. It was challenging and overwhelming, yet each instance brought me closer to hope.

CHAPTER 13
Caregiving and Burnout

"Solitude molds self-righteous people into gently, caring forgiving persons who are so deeply convinced of their own great sinfulness and so fully aware of God's even greater mercy that their life itself becomes ministry, in such a ministry there is hardly any difference left between doing and being. When we are filled with God's merciful presence, we can do nothing other than minister because our whole being witnesses to the light that has come into the darkness."

Henri Nouwen[28]

I never saw myself as a caregiver until the fall that followed Bryson's walk across the floor at his high school graduation, proudly holding a certificate of completion. On the day his brothers headed off to school, Bryson remained in bed. It struck me then: what would I do with him every day, all day? Since he was 2 years old, Bryson had been attending school – initially half-days for the first four years, and then a full eight hours each day. During those eight hours, someone else took charge, ensuring he accomplished all his activities, had lunch and looked out for his well-being. But now the responsibility fell solely on me.

My perception of caregiving was clouded with negativity from memories of my mom's caregiver journey. Let me tell you her story…..

As the school bus passed by her house, Wilma looked out with yearning. She felt the hope of her lifelong dream of graduating from high school and becoming a nurse fading away just as the bus did, slowly disappearing in the distance. She wanted to be the first in her family to graduate; none of her siblings had gone past the 10th grade, and she wanted to break the cycle. But here she was, looking out the window at home instead of heading off to start her senior year of high school.

It was a bittersweet moment, for she knew where her true priorities needed to be. Her younger sister, Joanna, needed her care, and her brother, John, was still home, too, requiring her attention and support.

Child number ten, the youngest of the brood, was Joanna. She was born with Down Syndrome. Joanna was six years younger than Wilma. Wilma's mother, Barbara, a woman of remarkable strength, was plagued with chronic asthma and a frail heart, rendering her incapable of strenuous labor. Wilma had lost three siblings, the third, eighth, and ninth in line, when they were at a young age. Theirs was a family that knew the true meaning of resilience.

As the bus passed the house on the day, Wilma's mother was in the hospital. She had fallen ill again from the illness that plagued her. Her older sisters had moved away, leaving Wilma with the weight of responsibility.

"Wilma, your mom and I have decided it will be best for her health if we leave Ohio and move to Arizona." Wilma's dad remarked a few months after the latest illness that had sent her mother to the hospital. Again, Wilma knew this was the best for her mother, but the sadness returned as she knew she would be saying goodbye to all her friends and letting go of all that she had ever known.

Wilma's heart sank with sadness as she pulled out of the driveway of the only house she had ever known, leaving with her mom, dad, and Joanna on the long drive across the country to Arizona. It had been heart-wrenching as they had said their goodbyes to family. Not knowing when they would see us again, also with the realization that this might be a final goodbye for her mother, whose health was always frail. She knew this was what was necessary, but at the young age of 18, she had her whole life ahead of her. It felt like this move was life-shaking.

In all of Wilma's mother's sicknesses, her foremost concern was the future of Joanna. It was a solemn responsibility for Wilma, with her mother not able to care for Joanna, to care for her younger sister. Her father, John was a pastor and he had to work to provide financially for the family.

Barbara fell seriously ill with the Asiatic flu several years after arriving in Arizona, with little hope of recovery. Wilma made a promise that would shape her future. She assured her mother that she would be the one to care for Joanna, no matter what. Sadly, her mother passed. At the age of 20, Wilma was left to fulfill her promise to her mother. It was a heavy burden, but Wilma carried it with grace and love.

As the years passed, Wilma and her father found a school in the Phoenix area that catered to Joanna's needs, offering her an opportunity to receive an education. This allowed Wilma to pursue her long-cherished dreams. She discovered a school that welcomed students without a high school diploma, and it was fortuitously the last year such an exception was allowed. With determination, Wilma went back to school, dedicating herself to becoming a Licensed Practical Nurse (LPN). It was a journey marked by hard work and sacrifice, but she was unwavering in her pursuit.

Several years later, Wilma's dad remarried, relieving her of her caregiving duties. Finally, she had the freedom to explore her own life beyond the responsibilities of her father and sister.

Wilma grabbed ahold of the freedom that she had been given. She didn't regret any of the past years of helping to care for her sister, but her entire life had been a sacrifice for helping in whatever ways she could with her mother's illnesses and Joanna's needs. She found opportunities of Bible school, voluntary service, and travels that eventually led her to meet the love of her life on a blind date. Her father, new stepmother, and Joanna also were given the opportunities of missions and serving. After the hardness of the early years, these years were a blessing from God.

Wilma became a wife and a mother. She had a close relationship with her parents and Joanna, but she didn't carry responsibility for their well-being. Fourteen years after receiving her freedom, her father, John, died suddenly of a heart attack. The shock that rippled through the community was huge. John had been a man of faith, a pastor, a friend to all. His love and care for his wife and Joanna had been incredible and now he was gone.

The love of her stepmother, Mary Ann (Deary), was amazing. She stepped in to care for Joanna and her needs, in a display of sacrifice and love. Being on the same property, Wilma found herself helping out more with Joanna's care, but she was not solely responsible. Sadly, ten years after she lost her father, Mary Ann died after a short battle with cancer. Joanna was now an orphan. It was clear as the only sibling that lived in the area, Wilma again needed to take the role of full-time caregiver and moved Joanna into their home. Wilma, as she had promised her mother many years before, would do everything to make sure that Joanna was okay. She stepped up and cared for her for the next 19 years until Joanna died at the age of 58 years old.

Caregiving isn't a duty, it's a true expression of love.

I had watched my mom struggle with the demands of being a wife, mother to two teenagers, and a caregiver for her sister. In addition to those roles, she worked part-time on the night shift at the local nursing home. Though I was young and couldn't fully grasp the depth of her caregiving roles, I could see the sacrifices she made. Every aspect of her life seemed devoted to giving, and she never complained.

Despite the challenges, she sacrificed and loved profoundly. It was evident in the sadness that lingered in her eyes when she heard of other couples enjoying outings or travel – experiences she felt alienated from due to her sister Joanna's needs.

Finding respite for Joanna was a constant struggle. Fortunately, several people stepped up to provide care for Joanna, allowing my parents occasional breaks. My father, equally devoted, joined my mom in their shared roles as providers and caregivers, ensuring the needs of Joanna, my brother, and me were met.

Tragically, 12 years after Joanna moved in with us, my amazing father died suddenly of a heart attack. The grief, shock, sadness, and hopelessness enveloped our family. The pillar of strength, security, and provider for my mom was gone. I was married and living nearby. My brother resided five hours away in Louisville. We couldn't fill the void. It was just Mom and Joanna, together but alone.

As I dealt with my father's death, thrust into responsibilities of the family business, and feeling the weight of being a helper for my mother, anger welled up within me. It seemed unfair. My parents planned to sell the business, find other placement for Joanna, and embark on travels and missions. Now, my mom's dreams ended tragically, and she was the sole caregiver.

My anger intensified as I observed my mom struggling to find space to grieve. Joanna required constant care, and I knew that her limited mental state made it challenging for her to process another close death in the family. Although moving Joanna wasn't a viable option, my mom desperately needed time. I vividly recall drafting letters to my mother's siblings, pouring out my soul about the injustice of her situation. I wanted to blame them for the hardship, and I was pouring out my own grief onto them. I disliked how life's twists had impacted my family. However, the letters were never sent. Despite the physical distance, my mom's siblings provided as much support as they could. At the early age of 56, my mother was a widow and a full-time caregiver, leaving me to wonder if she would ever catch a break.

Here I was at the age of 46, with the newfound responsibility of caring for Bryson all day, every day. "*God, what now?*" The uncertainty about Bryson's future loomed large, and I contemplated where he fit in this next stage of life. I desperately wanted to avoid experiencing what my mom had gone through. My fear of missing out on opportunities, much like my mom did, gripped me. I felt a sense of being stuck, realizing how the time when Bryson was in school had been a lifeline for me. The realization hit hard. Brad was always supportive, yet the dynamics of our family designated him as the primary breadwinner while I took the role of meeting Bryson's needs. In recent years, Brad has candidly shared that I didn't allow him to help as much as he wanted to. Although I would initially defend myself against this claim, the truth is I clung tightly to the control of Bryson's care until burnout set in. Admittedly, I brought this upon myself, but as a mother, the instinct to do everything possible for your child often takes over.

Fortunately, Bryson was able to access services through Vocational Rehab, securing a part-time job as a dietary assistant at a local college cafeteria, working sixteen hours a week. Additionally, he received community service hours through a waiver from the state, with a respite worker taking him out into the community one day a week. These support systems were a blessing, but they also meant my entire daily schedule revolved around coordinating Bryson's work and community service hours.

While my love for Bryson knew no bounds, the reality of the situation clashed with the expectations of what life was supposed to be. At this age, he should have been gaining independence, but instead, his friends headed off to college and other opportunities, leaving him feeling forgotten. I ventured into a new chapter of grief, left with a sense of isolation and entrapment.

By the time Bryson completed high school, I found myself in the worst mental state of my life. It had been two years since Stevan joined our family through adoption, and the challenges seemed insurmountable. I continued to see my therapist every two weeks, but just as we made progress in addressing one situation, a new challenge would emerge, throwing me off balance once again. It felt like I was constantly struggling to gain a firm grasp on my thoughts and emotions. Each new obstacle arose before I could fully navigate the previous one. Deep in depression, dealing with the trauma of our adopted son, coupled with the new responsibility of caring for Bryson 24/7, the future looked bleak, devoid of hope.

> **Dear brothers and sisters, when troubles of any kind come your way, consider it an opportunity for great joy. For you know that when your faith is tested, your endurance has a chance to grow. So let it grow, for when your endurance is fully developed, you will be perfect and complete, needing nothing.**
> **James 1:2-4**

The winter of 2019 brought an increased exhaustion from my caregiving duties. It wasn't just the physical aspect of having him at home and tending to his basic needs; I had also been managing his diabetic care for nearly 12 years. Feeling the weight, I embarked on a search for respite, not just to get away but to find solace. Despite being fortunate enough to travel with Brad and friends, I yearned for a retreat by myself or with someone who understood my situation. Hours spent on Google revealed a scant few resources for caregivers of children with disabilities, and none were conveniently located.

One cold, January day, I found myself wrapped up in my favorite blue fuzzy blanket on my recliner chair, seeking solace and I wrote in my journal.

My soul longs for peace and rest. My brain grumbles over the weight of life. The conflict between the two causes strife and anguish.

How do I find rest in this world? I like the idea of a cocoon; it's putting me in a padded cell at Oaklawn(our local mental hospital) where I can close myself off from the world. It seems peaceful, but I know I will never come out of there unless I change and let go. But how do I find a place to rest and change when life keeps moving on?

Frustration set in, and I found myself questioning the support from the church. What does the Bible say about caring for others? In my quest, I stumbled upon resources about sabbaticals for people in pastoral, leadership, and mission roles. The inequity struck me-Why could they take "time off" for three months to refresh and reclaim their souls, while mothers like me, who are caregivers 24/7 struggled to find a place for much-needed respite? It felt unfair in the opportunities for renewal and self-care.

While driving to Indianapolis one morning, taking Stevan to a doctor's appointment, I tuned in to a podcast featuring a well-known Christian music artist. She shared her experience of hitting a hard stop in life and being able to retreat to her family home, spending the summer solely focusing on her relationship with God and herself. Listening to her story, I couldn't help but feel a twinge of jealousy, and my anger boiled below the surface. Unlike her, I couldn't just get away by myself. I had a husband, four boys, and an extra dose of responsibilities that tethered me to my daily life.

Life isn't fair. I needed to get away.

"Lisa, you can take this money and use it for whatever you want," Brad said one wintery January morning in 2020. All I yearned for was a break. My mind raced back to the articles about sabbaticals that I had come across in my search. I decided to create a weekend sabbatical for my special needs moms' group.

I reached out to a friend with a lake house, hired another friend to assist with the meals, and enlisted my massage therapist to provide massages for all the weary moms. The first weekend of February, my Moms Need Moms group gathered. We attempted yoga, enjoyed delicious food, relaxed with massages, and completed puzzles as laughter filled the air. I left with a slightly lighter step, a sliver of hope, and a sense of being understood by other moms who shared similar journeys. It was a rejuvenating experience that fueled my spirit.

Only a few short weeks after the weekend sabbatical, COVID invaded our world. Bryson's job was gone, my two youngest boys, who were juniors in high school, were suddenly home. Reflecting on this, I chuckled to myself, thinking God knew I needed that brief weekend of refreshment because He knew what was coming ahead. Perhaps He was concerned about what I might do without the break.

True to my nature, I resolved to make the best out of the "stay at home order" from COVID. I immersed myself in planning themed events for the family and inventing work projects for the boys. While my intentions were good, the strain on my already weary mind, soul, and body made navigating the sudden craziness of the world extra challenging. However, I found my way, digging in and attempting to survive, as that was the only way I knew how to approach the chaos.

As I moved through the motions of my life, I felt the same trapped sensation that I had occasionally seen in my mother's eyes all those years as she cared for her sister. The future seemed unknown, and the daily responsibilities weighed heavily on me. I sensed grief, even if I couldn't quite put a name to it at the time. My mother, a saint and a warrior, had walked one foot ahead of the other in all the hardships. I aspired to be like her, to champion this life successfully, but I didn't want this challenge. It was a tug of war in my heart. I longed for assurance that something good would come out of this, and I yearned for an end to caregiving- a fulfilling future for my son that didn't involve his death.

Simultaneously, I didn't want my other children to bear the same caregiving burden my mother did with her sister. While I knew that they would be willing, as they have grown into strong men, it wasn't fair to impose this responsibility on them and their future families. Memories of my childhood resurfaced, sharing my mother with my aunt, and I couldn't bear the thought of doing the same to my future grandchildren. I knew I needed to find a way out of this caregiving role and a secure place for Bryson beyond our family.

In my despair, I continued to read and search for truth and insights that could lead me to freedom, whatever form it might take. That's when I stumbled upon this quote by Mike Mason: "I haven't the slightest doubt that God is bending over backward all day long to give me joy-but I must take it. Jesus stands at the crossroads, pointing the way to joy, inviting & encouraging, but I must choose. Lasting happiness comes only through choice, through the making of countless small decisions, one day at a time. Once I see this, it's not hard to choose. The hard part is admitting I have a choice."[29]

I realized I had a choice – to remain trapped and lost or to find freedom within myself, even if the circumstances in my life didn't change. Freedom can be found within heartache. Freedom can be found in the messiness of life. Freedom can be found in second chances. Freedom is a choice, and I wanted it. To attain this freedom, I knew I had to make the conscious decision to delve deep and do the internal work required to find it.

CHAPTER 14
Letting Go

You have been wandering around in this hill country long enough;
turn to the north.
Deuteronomy 2:3

As our younger children became the age to attend summer camps, Brad and I wrestled with what opportunities were in our area for Bryson. There were several disability camps in the area, but due to our choice to have Bryson in the mainstream in his education, we didn't think they would be the right choice for him.

It was 2010, and two years had passed since Bryson's life-changing diagnosis of Juvenile Diabetes. Through my network of other families walking the Diabetes journey, news of a Diabetes Camp about 45 minutes away from our home came to my attention. We believed it to be a perfect opportunity for Bryson to connect with other children facing the challenges of diabetes.

Bryson, however, exhibited little enthusiasm for this adventure. Reluctantly, he agreed to attend, and plans were set in motion. Truth to be told, I was looking forward to a reprieve from Bryson's care. I had booked a flight to Alberta, Canada, to spend time with my sisters-in-law while Bryson embarked on his camp journey. I wanted this experience for Bryson as much as I wanted a much-needed break.

The Sunday afternoon for Bryson's camp departure arrived, and as we finalized the packing of his belongings, I detected a flicker of fear in his eyes. "I'm not going," he shouted. I could feel anger rising to the surface. He sat down stubbornly on the bed in defiance. Brad and I approached the bed, and we knelt beside him, only to be assaulted with kicking of his feet. During this stage of his development, anger, and fear manifested in unpredictable kicks, pushes, or hits. "Bryson, we know you are scared, but this will be a great experience for you." "There will be other kids who have Diabetes like you." "You will get to play basketball and other fun activities." Brad and I kept repeating these phrases. For two hours, we stayed beside him, speaking, while Bryson continued to kick and declare he wasn't going. I could read the fear in his eyes, my mommy heart started to break, and doubt crept in. *Was this truly the right choice for my son?* I wanted to just give up and let Bryson stay home, but I also knew that this experience would be good for him. Selfishly, I knew I was going away, and I didn't want that to change.

After the grueling two hours, just shy of the camp check-in deadline, Bryson begrudgingly calmed down. Reluctantly, he got into the car, and we drove in silence, only with worship music playing during the 45-minute drive to camp.

Checking in and meeting his counselor proceeded smoothly, and Bryson appeared to adopt a reserved demeanor, obediently exploring the camp. We confided in the counselor about the tumultuous events at home, and reassurance was offered for a smooth transition.

As we walked away from his cabin to join the other campers in his cabin, Bryson suddenly realized our soon-to-be departure, and I saw a protective wall go up. Anticipating an emotional outburst, the counselor swiftly diverted Bryson's attention with an invitation to play basketball. Looking into Bryson's eyes, I said, "Go play basketball. You will enjoy playing. We will be here." He reluctantly walked away and started to play. What we did next still breaks my heart. We walked away and left him, with no goodbyes... we just left. The counselor knew what we were going to do and shielded Bryson from turning to see us. WE LEFT HIM...

Tears streamed down my face throughout the drive home and in the hours that followed. I sat in Bryson's room, my heart wrenched with loneliness and self-doubt. Questions tormented my mind - Had I scarred him? Would he resent us from leaving? Would he be okay? The ache in my heart was indescribable, a deep heart-wrenching cry echoed through my soul and poured out with wails of sadness. Yet, amidst the pain, the realization hit me – my role as his caregiver was all-encompassing, and the week without Bryson was an unexpected void. This was all new to me. Later that day, the camp called us and reassured us that Bryson had adapted well, and the next morning, I boarded a flight for my vacation.

Settling into the townhouse my sisters-in-law shared, I expressed my desire to simply read and relax. Knowing they both had to go to work, I anticipated having some much-needed alone time. I relished the opportunity for solitude, finding myself lingering in my pajamas well into the morning hours.

As I delved into Joyce Meyer's book, *Eat the Cookie... Buy the shoes: Giving yourself Permission to Lighten Up*, I found myself drawn to her humor within its pages, causing me to smile and chuckle to myself. But as I reached the final chapter, I realized that this book was far from a random selection. It seemed as though God had orchestrated its timing. In the chapter titled "Give Your Soul a Vacation," Meyer's words struck a chord with me: "You can take a vacation, thinking that you need a physical rest, but if you don't let your soul rest at the same time, you will return home just as exhausted as you were when you left."[30] And later, she emphasized, "Rest is not inactivity, but the harmonious working together of all the faculties and affection—of will, heart, imagination, and conscience."

These revelations were eye-opening for me. Here I was, away from home, on vacation, physically resting - but was I truly soul resting? This question lingered in my mind over the next few days. Evenings were filled with delicious food and heartfelt conversations with my sisters-in-law, and I was determined to ensure that this trip would yield positive results in my life.

Regrettably, Bryson's camp experience didn't end well. On Thursday, a call from Brad delivered unexpected news: "Bryson fell at camp. I need to go pick him up." My heart sank, and a cloud of self-blame enveloped me, I felt like a horrible mother. *I made Bryson go to camp, now look what happened.* Those next hours, I was a mess. I was the one who took Bryson to all his medical appointments, and I was the one there when he was sick. Did Brad know what to do? Here I was Bryson's primary caregiver, and I was thousands of miles away. I found myself agitated, just as I was beginning to grasp the concept of finding soul rest and striving for positive change, Bryson's situation threw a wrench into my plans. "God I don't understand," I cried out.

What seemed like forever, Brad finally called me again. "Bryson broke the bone in his upper right arm." "Again," I replied. This was the third time Bryson had broken his right arm. "We will get a cast put on tomorrow, he is doing good. Don't worry, keep enjoying yourself. I've got this." *Enjoy myself, how could I?* Did I really trust Brad to know what to do? Come to discover, Brad knew exactly what to do. He managed it all well!

This was a defining moment for me in multiple ways. I came to the realization that leaving was merely my attempt to escape the profound hurt and the ongoing struggle to accept my child with special needs. I understood that running away was not a solution; it wouldn't provide the soul rest that I desperately needed. Yet, in that moment of my journey, it was the only refuge I knew.

Moreover, I learned a valuable lesson about opening my clenched fists to trust that Brad and others could help Bryson, and that I needed to let go of the need to control every aspect of his care.

> "Sometimes fear does not subside, and one must choose to do it afraid."
> Elisabeth Elliot[31]

One evening, Bryson surprised me with a request: "Mom, can I go to the youth group retreat?" His words hung in the air. I felt a mix of surprise and uncertainty. While he wasn't actively involved in the weekly youth group activities, I knew he had several friends from school who also attended youth group at church.

"I'll have to check and see," was my cautious response, a habitual evasion of straightforward answers that had become the norm for me when Bryson sought permission for something. Memories of the trauma of Bryson attending Diabetes camp three years prior flooded my mind. The memories were vivid, and questions filled my mind: How would this work? Would someone in the youth group care enough to be his one-on-one buddy? I hoped, perhaps naively, that Bryson would forget about the retreat.

The following Sunday, the youth pastor caught me after church, "Lisa, we would love to have Bryson attend the youth retreat in a few weeks." I was humbled by his words. "I'm glad he wants to go, but apprehensive" I replied, "he would need a one-on-one buddy for the weekend." He immediately responded, " I will find someone to be his buddy." Gratitude swelled within me.

In the ensuing weeks, details fell into place – a buddy secured for Bryson. I yearned for Bryson to be just like any other teenager, and the youth group retreat was an opportunity to make that longing a reality. Yet, as the reality became real, my fears and unanswered questions heightened my anxiety. Unlike previous stays with Mamma or Diabetes Camp, where trained staff were present, this time, high school boys would be his companions. Would they be attentive enough? Could Bryson communicate his needs? Could he truly fit in? The struggle between my yearning for his normalcy and the truth of his differences and needs intensified. It was a battle within, a conflict between the little girl in me who wanted to fit in and a mother's heart who wanted the same for her son.

As the retreat weekend approached, a logistical challenge emerged. Bryson, the high school football team manager, could not leave at 4 pm with the bus and the rest of the kids because of the Friday night home football game. As questions arose in my head, a compassionate mother of a football player from the youth group reached out. "My boys will be happy to take Bryson to the retreat after the game." Relief washed over me at the demonstration of the love and care that I wished for my son.

Excitement radiated from Bryson as the game and the weekend drew near. I meticulously packed his belongings and organized a separate bag with labeled medications and diabetic supplies. Detailed instructions accompanied a list of areas where Bryson required assistance. I prayed his buddy would be thorough, relying on my spreadsheet for guidance.

There is something special about Friday night football under the lights. The evening air was cool and crisp, typical for late October. Although the game didn't end with a victory, I watched as Bryson, amidst disappointed players, completed his post-game duties. My emotions teetered on the edge – *could I truly let him go?* Insecurity and fears clawed at me, tempting me to call off the entire plan. I lingered just outside the fence. In that moment, I confronted a profound truth – my insecurities and fears were the barriers, not Bryson himself. It was a realization that hit me with a sobering understanding: I couldn't let my apprehensions steal away this potentially transformative experience from him. As he approached the fence, I said, "Bryson, have a good weekend. I have everything written down. Make sure you speak up if you need something, and call me if you need help." I rattled off. Bryson smiled, assuring me with an "Okay!" as he walked away with one of the players. As I headed to my vehicle, memories of walking away three years ago flooded my chest but this was different. Bryson was excited, happily walking away from me. I had to let go!

Letting Go

The weekend wasn't calm for me; thoughts of Bryson persisted. What were his blood sugars? How was he adapting to the overnight stay? Did he feel included? What if he has a seizure? The anxiety reached an unsustainable level by Saturday night. At my computer, I poured out my thoughts:

I must let go……. Yes, Bryson has limitations and is different in a lot of ways but me trying to protect him is not going to accomplish anything. I never thought Bryson would be able to have experiences like these, why am I struggling with this? I need to have an attitude adjustment and open my mind up to all the possibilities that my powerful and amazing God has for Bryson.

The youth retreat proved to be an outstanding experience for Bryson. Throughout the weekend, Bryson immersed himself in all of the activities and games. His dedicated buddy offered great support, teaching me an invaluable lesson of relinquishing some control and entrusting others to care for him.

"Bryson will live with me forever," echoed repeatedly in the sessions with my therapist. The profound depression that had gripped me since Stevan came to live with us was both exhausting and intense. The challenges of caregiving felt overwhelming, and I could only foresee negative outcomes for my future. The weight of the situation was all-encompassing, and the available living arrangements for Bryson seemed bleak. The idea of a group home was out of the question, and the prospect of an empty nest seemed unattainable. Our home, built in 2006, featured special accommodations in Bryson's room, our thought process was he would always live with us. It seemed like that was the only way our life could be, and I couldn't envision any other possibility.

In December 2019, a text message from Vicki lit up on my phone: "Do you want to meet for lunch?" The prospect excited me, and I swiftly replied with a resounding "Definitely." Vicki, a fellow special needs mom, had become an advocate for local parents battling the complexities of special education in the school system. Having recently lost her husband, I was eager to connect with her and see how she was navigating her new chapter of life.

Despite the cold, dreary December day, a craving for a Dairy Queen blizzard overcame me, and we decided to meet there for lunch. As we stood in line to order, our conversation flowed seamlessly, barely pausing to place our order before settling into the red booth seats. In the initial moments, we caught up on the sudden changes life had thrown Vicki with the loss of her husband and partner in their shared journey of parenting children with disabilities. Their decision to adopt three children with disabilities, guided by the Holy Spirit, had created a loving home.

Vicki began sharing about their plans before her husband's death, "Carl and I were planning to move to Arizona in a few years. Arizona has the best disability benefits." She went on to explain, "They offer Adult Development homes. It's like a foster home but for adults with disabilities, they live with a family." My curiosity piqued, and I bombarded her with questions.

The mention of Arizona struck a chord of personal connection for me. It wasn't just a state on the map; it held layers of significance. My mother had once called it home during her young adult years. I had relatives residing in the area. Brad and I served there on a three-month mission shortly after our marriage. Moreover, our frequent travels were often prompted by the fact that my lifelong friend, Lyn, and her family had moved to Phoenix several years prior. The Chicago Cubs played spring training there. Bryson had developed a keen obsession with the idea of moving there as well. Given this rich history, the information Vicki shared about Adult Development homes in Arizona deeply intrigued me.

The news about Arizona's exceptional benefits for individuals like Bryson sparked a glimmer of hope. Perhaps there was another path, another possibility. However, Vicki's next words tempered my hope.

"I can't move there anymore without Carl. I need to stay where I have my village," she confided. My heart broke for her as I realized the loss of her dreams, but I knew she needed the support she found in her current surroundings.

Despite the bittersweet turn in our conversation, we continued chatting for over two hours. Vicki's journey, albeit marked by heartbreaking circumstances, left me with a heart full of encouragement. The strength and resilience she displayed in navigating such challenges was truly inspiring.

Seated by my computer that evening, my go-to place for research, I dove deep into the world of possibilities. Googling Arizona Benefits, Adult Development Homes, and various related terms, page after page of information unfolded. Excited about one website, I promptly emailed my friend Lyn in Arizona, eager to share my discoveries. Lyn's response echoed excitement, proclaiming, "Let's get the Pletts to move to Arizona, too!" While a glimmer of hope lingered, the sheer magnitude of the challenge made it seem impossible.

Just a few weeks after my conversation with Vicki, Lyn sent an email about a Christian agency in Phoenix dedicated to working with adults with disabilities. Her friends knew the co-founders and praised their passion for securing the best opportunities for their clients. Intrigued, I sent an email to Barbara, one of the founders, for more information. Her response arrived several days later, offering her resources for any assistance I might need.

The possibility of Bryson living away from me lingered in my thoughts. Each time I dared to discuss these prospects during my therapy appointments, my therapist would gently probe. She would challenge me to explore why I felt that way, asking me to question the truth behind my assertions. Invariably, my response had been, "There is no hope."

As the idea of moving Bryson to Arizona grew more intense in my mind, I became increasingly aware that fear was the driving force behind my thoughts. During one Monday morning therapy appointment, I immediately broached the subject of Arizona again. I shared my thoughts: I don't know if I can do this. I know that fear is holding me back, and I know that I have to do this! She helped me wrestle with each of these aspects, prompting me to clarify my feelings as clarity began to emerge. I felt my emotions begin to calm, and a subtle glimmer of possibility began to surface. I realized that I could do this - I could let go of my fears and make the decision to move my son to Arizona.

Over the course of several years, a continuous exchange of emails traveled between us and the agency. I traveled to the Phoenix area and visited current Adult Development Home (ADH) homes. Bryson, ever optimistic, continued to share with everyone he met - he was moving to Arizona. The move seemed possible, but my mind struggled with the multitude of details and the sheer enormity of the idea.

The vastness of it all felt overwhelming. I was fatigued and burned out, and while I yearned for a respite, the idea of navigating the seemingly difficult process loomed overhead. Did I have the energy to work and fight with what it might all entail? Did I genuinely want to let Bryson go, relocating him 1900 miles, no less? The notion was appealing, but the practicalities of our family business anchored us in Indiana. Unsure of how it would unfold, Brad recognized the urgency that something needed to change for me.

After much prayer and discussion, we decided the ADH "Adult Development Home" concept felt like the right fit. On August 12, 2021, I emailed Barbara at the agency: "Brad and I talked last night. We feel like transitioning Bryson to an adult development home is the right fit for him at this time. Please let me know what you need to start the process." The path forward remained uncertain, but this declaration signaled the start of a journey we were willing to undertake, one step at a time.

As Bryson continued to express his dream of moving to Arizona several weeks after our decision, we shared the good news with him. "Bryson, we are talking with people in Arizona about you moving there. Isn't that exciting news?" His response was muted, but it was evident he was processing the information. The next few months, as we explored potential providers for Bryson and we shared the news with him, the frequency of his conversations about moving to Arizona dwindled.

One November afternoon, driving home from his job at the local college cafeteria, Bryson seemed restless. It was apparent he wanted to share something but struggled to find the words. Finally, in a quiet voice, he said, "I had water in my eyes today." Concerned, I asked, "Why, Bryson, what's the matter?" He hesitated before revealing, "I am scared about moving to Arizona." Instantly, I felt my hands tighten their grip on the steering wheel as if trying to anchor myself. My mind was reeling, feeling as though it had just been struck with a heavy blow. Bryson wasn't one to openly share his feelings, and his method of processing change differed from the norm. For him to voice his fear marked a significant moment. I understood the importance of staying calm when I responded to him, "Bryson, it's ok to be scared. We will figure this out," I reassured him.

Confronted with Bryson's newfound fears, uncertainty gripped me. I immediately dialed Brad after I returned home, my voice tainted with fear and frustration, "What do we do, stop?" Brad, ever composed, responded, "He needs to process. Give him time. Let's just slow the process down." Reluctantly, I reached out to Barbara via email, outlining Bryson's fears. In her reassuring reply, she offered solace, "Lisa, please do not worry. We will collaborate with you and do everything we can to assist with the transition so Bryson does not feel stressed or anxious." Her words provided much-needed reassurance. The plan to pause and focus on Bryson's concerns was forefront in our minds.

Waiting is not merely about passing time; it's about trusting the process and believing that something beautiful is on the horizon.

"Lisa, one of our customers that we are building a house for, has a 5th wheel RV for sale," Brad shared one evening in late April 2022. As we both sat in our home office, engrossed in our laptops, "What if we would buy the RV, and you and Bryson live in that as you transition him to Arizona." The topic had been untouched during the past four months. The notion lingered in my mind as I struggled with the daily responsibilities of caring for Bryson. Though the logistics seemed taunting, Brad's proposal intrigued me. I wasn't fond of living in an RV, but the financial benefits made practical sense. After several weeks of contemplation, I emailed Barbara, "We are moving ahead with the process. We have had some great talks with Bryson, and he is calm and ready for it. We are purchasing an RV, and Bryson and I will be moving out there at the beginning of October." The plan was set in motion, and we were determined to make this happen.

October 2022 was the start of letting go. To reach the destination I yearned for, I had to dig deeper into myself and find my inner strength. Here I was, preparing to live across the country, something I once deemed impossible. As I reflected on the process of bringing Stevan into our family, I wondered, *Would letting Bryson go be just as challenging?* For 25 years, mothering and caring for Bryson had defined my life and identity. Much of the journey with Bryson felt like a solo endeavor – just Bryson and me. While Brad was always present, my commitment from the beginning to do everything in my power to ensure Bryson had all he needed, the need for control had put me in that place.

Although I was burned out and exhausted, yearning for a break, The goal of this move was to grant me a respite, a release from the role of being his caregiver, and to pave the way for his future. To make that happen, Brad, in his role as the family provider, would stay in Indiana and continue to work. It would be just Bryson and me, embracing the next chapter in the desert of Arizona.

The initial few weeks in the remote RV resort, residing in a 5th wheel trailer, felt like a vacation – a brief escape from reality. However, as time progressed, the challenges began to surface. Personal space was in short supply. Amidst the beautiful surroundings, I was overloaded with logistics - applications to fill out, and phone calls to make. I was provided names of Adult Development providers (ADH) interested in welcoming Bryson into their homes. Processing through each provider's biography and arranging interviews became a significant part of each day.

Amidst the planning, there was ample time for me to reflect. Many sleepless nights led me to ponder, "*What in the world am I doing in the middle of the desert with my oldest son and finding him a family to live with 1900 miles away from me?*" Memories from my teenage years resurfaced, the label of "rebel" and the internalized belief that my actions were constantly being watched by others, I rolled the question over and over in my mind, "*What are people going to say about what we are doing?*" brought uncertainty and cast doubt on the path that we had chosen.

One evening Bryson and I attended Elevation Worship with Stevan Furtick concert. It was powerful but it also stirred up more wrestling in my spirit. I journaled that night back at the RV.

God performs miracles... I believe He does! God has His plans and purposes for us... I believe He does! He knows what is best for me.... I believe He does! I believe in the power of prayer... I believe He answers prayers! When I pray and wait on Him to answer, I feel my anxiety rise and I KNOW I need to surrender to His timing.... So, what do I do now?? Do I pray without ceasing.... The Word says to do that! Do I surrender it to Him and lay down my worries and let His timing be His timing? So how do I pray without ceasing and ask for a miracle and wait and surrender and be calm all at the same time?

Thankfully, I had worked through a lot of the trauma of Stevan's adoption process and adoption, but I felt, at times, I was in the same place I had been many years before, wanting to believe God, wanting to trust, wanting to pray, but struggling with it all. I knew deep down that it was the right course for both Bryson and me.

The journey – undoubtedly right, yet undeniably challenging.

One afternoon, as I sat outside, basking in the warmth of the sunshine, the majestic mountains painting a breathtaking backdrop. Despite the beauty surrounding me, my heart carried a weight, and in that moment, I wrote these words....

When there is beauty all around you, but your soul remains sad
When you see the goodness of Jesus, but your heart still is heavy
When you know He has plans for you, but you feel there is nothing to dream
When you can see the reflection of God's amazing beauty all around you, but your eyes are void of life
When you are surrounded by people, but you still feel all alone
When you can look up at the mountains, know where your help comes from, but you feel like the climb is too hard to do
When you know, God has every minute of your day in His control, but the day seem long, and the nights even longer

The months of waiting for approval felt long and unrelenting. In the separation from my home, husband, the rest of my family, and my friends, I clung to every shred of hope to endure the challenges and loneliness. The promise of a better future sustained me, but the present was undeniably difficult.

One Sunday afternoon, as Bryson and I drove from church back to the RV, we encountered several lane closures due to a bike race. For 13 miles, we drove alongside the bikers, witnessing their endurance and determination. Some pushed north with a slight incline, while others were already on their way south. Intrigued by the event, I googled it and discovered it was Ironman Arizona. The sheer magnitude of the competition fascinated me- It began with a 3.8 km (2.36 miles) swim, followed by a grueling 180 km (111.85 miles) bike ride, and concluded with a challenging 42.2 km (26.2 miles) run. Approximately 2500 athletes participated in this remarkable feat.

In the following days, the images of these bikers and the word "endurance" continued to echo in my mind. The definition of endurance - *the ability to withstand hardship or adversity; the ability to sustain a prolonged stressful effort or activity.* Or another definition - *the act or an instance of enduring or suffering.*[32]

As I thought about the definition, I realized the reality of endurance is hard and long. Why would individuals willingly subject themselves to this physical and mental strain? They signed up, paid the entrance fee, and knew precisely what awaited, yet they showed up. Personally, I'm not an athlete, and my physical status has never been described as "in shape." While I have participated in several 5k runs and walks and had phases of regular exercise, I lack any "athletic mentality." I couldn't relate to willingly undertaking something as strenuous as the Ironman competition.

Yet, I felt a powerful connection to this race and the words "hard" and "long." It felt like my life's journey. The internal struggle lay in the fact that I hadn't agreed to this; I hadn't signed up for it. On that cold January morning in 1998, when a nurse informed me of Bryson's seizure in the nursery, I was unprepared and had no choice but to show up and become the best mom to my first-born son.

Is this endurance... living in an RV in the middle of the desert, 1900 miles from home...searching for a family for Bryson to live with? Does it capture the ability to withstand hardship and sustain a prolonged stressful effort? The word "endurance" carried a weight of negativity as I reflected on the 24 years and ten months of caring for Bryson – it had indeed been hard and long.

Endurance became the core of our journey in the desert of Arizona – a hard and long path. Bryson was denied placement into the Adult Development Home (ADH) by the state due to his Diabetes, encountering perplexing obstacles. In standard Lisa form, I fought tirelessly, wrote letters and emails, made phone calls, and even hired a lawyer. The experience was full of challenges that seemed impossible, yet in the end, God provided what we needed. Seven and a half months after Bryson and I moved to Arizona, he found his new home with a family perfectly suited for him- a family that, after the first meeting, both Bryson and I knew was exactly right. God orchestrated the perfect solution.

Reflecting on the Ironman athletes who willingly signed up for a grueling 7 to 12-hour race despite knowing the hardships they would face, I draw parallels to my own race. While I was exhausted at the "finish line" of transitioning Bryson and letting go, a realization hit. The weariness didn't diminish the beauty of the experience. Despite caregiver fatigue, the physical and mental demands, and the constant worry about Bryson's future, the process held a unique beauty.

Back in 1998, I didn't anticipate the challenges that lay ahead, but I faced them with a strength that mirrors the Ironman race. Would I do it over again? The answer is a resounding yes. Bryson has shown me beauty in a new way- his courage, strength, and acceptance of his disabilities. His positive outlook on life has forged countless wonderful memories. I love my son wholeheartedly, embracing every quirk, thought, and passion. As I released the caregiving role to someone else… I discovered the profound privilege of simply being Bryson's mom!

CHAPTER 15
Hope and Healing

"Sometimes you have to let go of the picture of what you thought life would look like and learn to find joy in the story you are actually living."
Rachel Marie Martin[33]

It was a frigid, snowy January morning, a palpable sense of struggle enveloped me. The relentless winter in Northern Indiana, courteous of the perma-cloud from Lake Michigan, hid the sun for days on end. I struggled with recent hardships, desperately seeking joy. As the water cascaded over me in the shower, I questioned God, "What do you want me to do with this pain?" I listened intently for His voice. Though His guidance wasn't conveyed in audible words, it was undeniably clear. "Who are you, Lisa?"

His question hung in the air as the steam of the shower hovered. I hadn't contemplated my identity this way before. Once dressed, I made my way to the computer. There, I opened a blog I had started-a personal journal, its entries meant for my eyes alone. As the blog appeared on my screen, my attention turned to the blog description:

I am the wife to a wonderful man, Brad, and the mother of three incredible young men; Bryson age 11, Tyrell age 9 and Kaden age 6. My heart is passionate about my God, my family, my church and my community. I am busy with my involvement in these areas. God has brought me on an awesome journey so far in my life, and I can't wait to see what He has in store!!!

Seated at my computer, I pondered the words, realizing that my written description wove my identity into my roles and involvements. A memory surfaced from a Beth Moore study on Esther,[34] where she emphasized the tendency to disconnect or erase aspects about ourselves or our past. Beth encouraged us to embrace those parts because they might be the link to God's plan. Recalling that message, I connected it to the moment in the shower when God had questioned me, "Who are you, Lisa?"

In that contemplative space, I knew what God wanted me to acknowledge. With a soft, hesitant voice, I spoke the words I had avoided: "I'm a mother of a special needs child." Saying it aloud felt uncomfortable. I had attempted to bury it. I didn't want it to be true. Yet, in that moment, a subtle shift occurred within me. This admission came 11 years into the journey with Bryson. The utterance brought a shift in my spirit, marking a new level of healing.

After Bryson's graduation, he enjoyed the company of Ed, a wonderful older gentleman, as his community worker every Monday. Their routine involved exploring various parks during long walks and ensuring Bryson received exercise and fresh air, which were my main goals. Additionally, they would dine at different restaurants, where Ed took the opportunity to impart essential life skills to Bryson. Ed, with extensive experience in the realm of disabilities, would often share stories upon their return, drawing parallels between Bryson and another young man he had worked with who had Autism.

In September 2022, during Bryson's annual neurological appointment, I requested a letter detailing his diagnosis for Bryson's application, applying for benefits in our move to Arizona. As the nurse reviewed Bryson's records, she printed out a summary of the day's assessment, including his diagnoses. The document listed seizures, right-side hemiplegia, generalized Cerebral Palsy, and surprisingly, AUTISM SPECTRUM DISORDER! This revelation left me in shock, as the term had never been mentioned in his 24 years and eight months of seeing various neurologists.

The weight of this newfound information hit me, and I couldn't help but think about the potential services Bryson might have received had I known and advocated for ASD earlier. Shortly after our move to Arizona, I discussed Bryson's behaviors with the agency staff assisting me in the transition. After a brief conversation with Bryson, the staff member, drawing from years of experience in the disability field, made a bold statement about Bryson, "He displays many traits of Autism." While not totally surprising, this direct affirmation from another knowledgeable source felt like the missing piece of a puzzle, offering a clearer understanding of Bryson's disability.

Later that evening, after the staff member mentioned the word "Autism" to me, I decided to explore further by typing "autism symptoms" into my Google search. The results were overwhelming, flooding me with information that seemed to perfectly align with some of Bryson's behaviors. My son has Autism. Creating a spreadsheet, I meticulously listed symptom after symptom, detailing how each one applied to Bryson personally. The process, though draining, brought a unique sense of freedom and understanding. It's truly remarkable how a new diagnosis can bring a sense of healing. While it doesn't alleviate the challenges and frustrations associated with his "autistic characteristics," having a name for it provided a sense of clarity and helped dispel the feeling of being alone.

In the fall of 2021, I volunteered to help my sister-in-law clear out her family's estate. They were collectors, hoarders. I was captivated by what I might find in the next box. As I started the process, I had a tough time wrapping my head around how someone could keep so much stuff. I looked up the definition and found that it is a psychological disorder of not being able to get rid of things.

As I started the huge task, thankfully, the boxes were labeled – kitchen stuff, books, magazines, bottles, trains, fabric, crafts and the list went on and on. I, along with several friends, spent many evenings and weekends sorting through the labeled boxes. One evening, I was exhausted, but my mind couldn't shut off. I felt that God brought to my mind the boxes that I had labeled and stored away – overweight, conservative, shy, fear, trust, Bryson, my dad, Stevan, grief, anger, church, rules, and busyness. I had many boxes that I needed to unpack.

Oh, how I wanted to unpack those boxes, but unpacking is HARD. Do I start with the newest boxes, the ones that are right in front of me, or do I dig and go back to the ones in the back corner that are hiding? I realized that was what I had been doing for many years. I didn't know where to start in dealing with the issues that haunted me, so I did nothing. I let the boxes sit and pile up. I kept collecting, stuffing, and hoarding.

It seems that Satan keeps us bound by urging us to hoard our hurts, memories, and pain. God, on the other hand, desires us to be free in Him, to trust and rely on Him. We often block off our hearts, shut down our emotions, and cling to the very things that keep us from experiencing real life and true freedom in Christ. These emotional roadblocks create a false sense of safety.

I started therapy by seeing a spiritual director. Her gentle spirit and reassuring presence was a balm for my soul. I shared with her many of my struggles and fears. She brought me into the presence of my loving heavenly Father in prayer. It was a beautiful experience, but when my world started spinning out of control during the adoption process, I realized that I needed more professional, psychological help.

As I write this book, I have been seeing the same incredible therapist for nine years. Under her guidance, we began the process of unpacking each of those labeled boxes. We used many different tools over the years to unpack. Together, we worked with the IFS (Internal Family Systems)[35], used EMDR[36] therapy and also studied the Enneagram.[37] Each of these tools played a critical role in uncovering the contents of the boxes I had carried for so long.

The most impactful aspect of therapy for me was having a safe place where I could simply be myself, knowing that I would be heard without judgment. Through this process, I also learned how to genuinely care for myself, and one crucial aspect of this was finding the right depression/anxiety medication that suited my body.

I also uncovered that my understanding of faith and God lacked a personal dimension. It was entangled with rules and labels, a web that dictated what I should and shouldn't do. The belief was that my salvation required work, and I had to be a good girl.

This distorted view extended to my approach to Bryson's life. Fueled by my insecurities, fears, and pride, I viewed him through the filter of "not fitting in." My lifelong struggle with weight, and the lingering memory of a prayer uttered in desperation, "God, anything but a handicapped child," further shaped my narrative and influenced every decision I made.

As I started to unpack these deep-seated beliefs, I realized the extent to which I hadn't truly lived. While I had shed the "physical" rules, my mind remained imprisoned by judgments, rules and labels, and external expectations. In the process of therapy and unpacking the boxes/beliefs, I unearthed the real me, buried deep beneath all the boxes. I realized I could throw out the trash, the words NOT ENOUGH, UNWORTHY, OVERWEIGHT, GOOD GIRL, AFRAID. This journey allowed me to claim my freedom and embrace a more authentic and freer version of myself.

The journey of acceptance and healing did not provide answers to all my "why" questions. It didn't shield me from more moments of grief, and there are still days when I crumble in hopelessness. Acceptance, much like grief, is a gradual process, requiring the peeling off of layer after layer of self-erected walls to dig deep into the raw reality of life.

Choosing acceptance meant finding hope daily, claiming truth, and recognizing the purpose of my story. The truth has always been present, but I needed to discover the person I was beneath it all. Bryson's life and the adoption of Stevan became vehicles through which I discovered my true self. God orchestrated through His grace and mercy the lessons I needed to learn.

Without the difficult, the hard, the questioning, would I have reached out for counseling? Through this process, I unraveled the root cause of my struggles: I didn't feel like I was ENOUGH, I didn't feel SAFE, I didn't feel KNOWN. These insecurities fueled my internal battles each time a situation with Bryson arose. Therapy provided me with a fresh perspective, offering valuable tools to analyze, process, ponder, and reshape how I viewed Bryson, myself, others, and even God.

In recent years, I've been gradually emerging from that dark and hard place as a transformed person.... more free, more whole... While the external situations haven't changed; I'm still a mother of a special needs son, I still have an adopted son, I'm still overweight, my mother is still a widow, I'm still involved in our family business, I find myself learning to dig through more of the internal boxes. I'm becoming adept at recognizing the distracting voices. Though still broken and not always feeling strong, I am stronger for having experienced grace and hope. I bear witness to the unique and beautiful way God works in our lives.

God, in His infinite wisdom, employs life's trials to foster growth and strength within us. His constant presence guides us through each hardship. Years ago, I began questioning: "Am I willing to stand in the midst of adversity, looking different and finding peace because God has placed me here for this time and for this purpose?" I am drawing closer to being able to answer my question with a resounding yes and to fully comprehend the nature of my ministry. While questions may persist until I reach Heaven, I am confident that God's plans are ultimately for my good. The ongoing challenge is to embrace these purposes and let God use them for His glory. As Rick Warren states, "Other people are going to find healing in your wounds. Your greatest life messages and your most effective ministry will come out of your deepest hurts."[38]

Beauty lies in our heartache. Beauty lies in the mess of life. Beauty lies in the second chances. Beauty lies in freedom. Beauty lies in Jesus.

My family of six is a unique tribe, a blend of Canadian, American, and Jamaican roots. We embrace our individual quirks and special needs; some more apparent than others. In our family, you'll find variations of height, size, shape, and color reflecting our diversity . Yet through it all, we are united. This family has been the driving force behind my therapeutic journey. It is for them that I sought to find hope and healing.

As I began to comprehend my identity in Christ and fully embrace myself, I found the capacity to accept Bryson and the extraordinary path God charted for us. Bryson experienced a stroke before he was born. God knew him intimately even before his birth. God was fully aware of me as well, fully cognizant of the boxes I held onto tightly. With His perfect plan in mind, God transformed what was a difficult, terrifying event - a stroke- into something beautiful, both in Bryson and in myself. Indeed, He has continually revealed His love for both Bryson and me, time and time again. The most significant reward in this ongoing process is the realization that God is my hope, the reason I live and breathe. His hope has carried me through, and it continues to propel me forward. Through a Stroke of Love, I found the ultimate Hope!

I prayed to the Lord, and he answered me. He freed me
from all my fears. Those who look to him for help will be
radiant with joy; no shadow of shame
will darken their faces.
In my desperation I prayed, and the Lord listened; he saved
me from all my troubles.
For the angel of the Lord is a guard; he surrounds and
defends all who fear him.
Taste and see that the Lord is good. Oh, the joys of those
who take refuge in him!
Psalm 34:4-8

Acknowledgements

This book is a testament to the unwavering support and encouragement of my family and friends. I am deeply grateful for each of you who walked beside me on the journey.

Brad – You have always been there for me, and I know there were days you had had enough. As an Enneagram 9, your calmness, accepting and stable demeanor, and your open mindedness, was a huge piece of my healing. I am very thankful God gave me a hockey loving Canadian Farmer. I love you!

Tyrell, Stevan and Kaden – thanks for your support and encouragement during the writing process. So many of these experiences you were a part of but so young to comprehend. I am sorry for the times I wasn't present or kind as I dealt with the hard parts of this journey. I am proud of the unique relationship each of you shares with Bryson. Your love for him shines brightly. I love each of you uniquely as you are!

Bryson – Though you may never read these words, you taught me invaluable lessons. I love you and the journey we have shared.

Fran – I'm sure you didn't want to be "featured" in this book. But there wasn't a way to tell my story without you. You have been my constant friend, and I'm grateful you have stayed on course. I'm blessed to have you and your amazing family in my life.

Lynette & Gordon – Thank you Lynette for being my cheerleader and for blessing me with your beautiful spirit. Words cannot express how deeply grateful for the warmth and love your family has extended to Bryson since he was young. Thank you for "adopting" him as your son in Arizona.

Moms Need Moms group - Thank you for the unwavering support and encouragement through the years. Our times together provided a safe place for me. Your resilience in confronting the toughest challenges with your children fills me with pride. Remember, you are strong and beautiful.

COS group – The way we made our initial connection as a group was truly a God thing. Our deep conversations have been lifelines during difficult times. Thanks for your prayers and always being there when I needed you.

6-Pack - Our vacations together were like a breath of fresh air, offering Brad and me a precious opportunity to escape life's challenges and simply unwind, sharing laughter and relaxation. The unwavering support and understanding we've received from all of you over the years has truly fortified our marriage, and for that, I'm incredibly grateful.

Mom - You have been my anchor and my biggest fan. Thank you for all the physical help and yummy food you have provided over the years. I know your life has been hard, but you never stopped serving and giving because of it, and I'm forever grateful. I love you.

Hope*Books team – Thank you for believing in my dream of writing a book and for making it a reality. To my May Cohort author friends, your advice, encouragement and support is what kept me moving ahead in this process. I am grateful that this book has connected us and I'm cheering each of you on in your process of publishing your Hope stories.

Acknowledgements

Therapist Tanya – Your guidance and wisdom were instrumental in my journey of self-discovery. Thank you for encouraging me to keep moving forward in those dark days.

Ultimately, I am grateful to God Almighty. His grace, patience, and kindness gave me the courage to heal and find hope!

Endnotes

1. Helen Keller and Kelly Wester Anderson, The Story of My Life (Createspace Independent Publishing Platform, 2017)
2. Brainyquote.com/quotes/albert_einstein_390808
3. Jerico Silvers • Writings (@jericosilvers) • Instagram photos and videos
4. Welcome To Holland — Emily Perl Kingsley
5. **C.S. Lewis,** *Letters to Malcolm, Chiefly on Prayer* (HarperOne, 2017)
6. Henri Nouwen, *Bread for the Journey: A daybook of wisdom and faith* (HarperOne, 2006)
7. Mary Ann Radmacher, *Courage doesn't always Roar* (Conari Press, 2009)
8. www.goodnewsnetwork.org/theodore-roosevelt-quote-on-courage
9. 20 Inspirational Family Quotes (yourpositiveoasis.com)
10. The Parents' Review - AmblesideOnline - Charlotte Mason Curriculum
11. What Is an IEP? Individualized Education Programs, Explained (edweek.org)
12. Vierstra, Gretchen, and Brittney Newcomer. "Paraprofessionals: What you need to know." *Understood.org*, https://www.understood.org/en/articles/paraprofessionals-what-you-need-to-know
13. Individuals with Disabilities Education Act (IDEA)
14. Henri J. M. Nouwen, *Adam God's Beloved* (Orbis; Anniversary edition (November 3, 2022)
15. S.D. Gordon, Quiet Talks on Prayer (CreateSpace Independent Publishing Platform, 2017)
16. (2) Christine Caine - When we respond in obedience to God's Word,... | Facebook
17. Craig Groeschel, *Weird, because Normal isn't working* (Zondervan, 2011)

18. https://www.christiantoday.com/article/john-wesley-10-quotes-on-faith-evangelism-and-putting-god-first/89402.htm
19. https://www.azquotes.com/quote/1121824
20. Helen Keller and Kelly Wester Anderson, *The Story of My Life (Createspace Independent Publishing Platform, 2017)*
21. 21 Inspirational First Time Mom Quotes - Strong With Grace
22. C.S. Lewis, *The Four Loves*(HarperOne, 2017)
23. Brainyquotes.com/authors/misty-copeland-quotes
24. The Life of Power to Follow (utmost.org)
25. Marianne Williamson, *A Return to Love: Reflections on the Principles of "A Course in Miracles"* (HarperOne, 1996)
26. Henri J.M. Nouwen, edited by Michael Ford, A dance of Life: Weaving Sorrows and blessings into One Joyful Step (Ave Maria Pr January 1, 2006)
27. Victor Frankl, *Man's Search for Meaning* (Beacon Press, 2006)
28. Henri Nouwen, *Out of Solitude: Three Meditations on the Christian Life* (Ave Maria Press, 30th Anniversary ed.(October, 2004)
29. Mike Mason, *The Mystery of Marriage: Meditations on the Miracle* (Multnomah: Anniversary edition (June, 2005)
30. Joyce Meyer, Eat the Cookie… Buy the Shoes: Giving yourself Permission to Lighten Up (Faithwords, April 2010)
31. Elisabeth Elliot - Sometimes…fear does not subside and…one must… (bibleportal.com)
32. www.merriam-webster.com
33. Rachel Marie Martin, *Mom Enough: Inspiring Letters for the Wonderfully Exhausting but Totally Normal Days of Motherhood* (Dexterity, September 2023)
34. Beth Moore, Esther – *Bible Study Book: It's tough Being a Woman* (Lifeway Press, 2008)
35. Internal Family Systems Therapy | Psychology Today
36. What is EMDR? - EMDR Institute - EYE MOVEMENT DESENSITIZATION AND REPROCESSING THERAPY
37. www.enneagraminstitute.com
38. Rick Warren, The Purpose Driven Life: What on Earth am I Here For? (Zondervan, 10th Edition (October, 2012)

www.ingramcontent.com/pod-product-compliance
Lightning Source LLC
Chambersburg PA
CBHW020245010526
44107CB00002B/104